After-Dinner Laughter

Favorite Stories of the Famous & Not-So-Famous

Introduction by PRINCE PHILIP

Edited by SYLVIA L. BOEHM

Illustrated by BRIAN BLAKE

 STERLING PUBLISHING CO., INC. NEW YORK

Library of Congress Catalog Card No.: 76-51166
Sterling ISBN 0-8069-0102-0 Trade
0103-9 Library

Publisher's Note

Ever since Chaucer's "Canterbury Tales" was published, collections of anecdotes have been popular, especially humorous ones.

This collection was gathered from leading British after-dinner speakers who were asked to contribute their favorite stories for the Oxfam charitable organization in Great Britain. It shows American readers (and speakers) that the English sense of humor should not be underrated but laughed with. This is especially apparent with after-dinner speakers who always seem to spark up even the dreariest banquet or dinner party with their personal little jokes and tales.

All royalties to the book are being paid to the Oxfam movement. If you would like to know the names of the contributors, please turn to the appendix where their names and titles are listed, as well as a description of what Oxfam is.

We hope this book will not only amuse you but give you a store of jokes in case you are called on to speak anywhere.

A speaker once proposed a toast to my health in terms rather more generous than usual and to cap it all quoted these two lines from John Dryden:-

"A man so various that he seemed to be
Not one but all mankind's epitome."

Fortunately I had seen a draft of his speech before he made it and I was able to look up the quotation before replying. So in responding to the toast I was able to say:-

"Some people might well feel that he has succeeded in presenting me not just in a good light but in a positively rosy glow of perfection. I can only imagine that he has taken Disraeli's advice that 'Everyone likes flattery; and when you come to Royalty you should lay it on with a trowel'. At any rate I hope that what he has left unsaid is not an indication of his true feelings, because the rest of the quotation from Dryden, which he carefully left out, goes like this:-

Stiff in opinions, always in the wrong
Was everything by starts and nothing long;
But in the course of one revolving moon
Was chemist, fiddler, statesman and buffoon."

1 **A High Sheriff tells this story:**

A psychiatrist, receiving a new patient, observed that she carried under her arm a live duck. However, being accustomed to idiosyncrasies he made no comment, and, asking her to be seated, inquired what he could do for her.

"Oh, it's not I who need help, doctor," she replied, "it's my husband here, he thinks he's a duck."

2 **This is a business executive's favorite story:**

Army was playing Navy in their annual football game. No bigger or more enthusiastic crowd ever packed the stadium; the seats had been sold out weeks ahead. But what should Joe Davies see next to his neighbor Mr. Jones, but one empty seat.

"Mr. Jones," he exclaimed, "you have an empty seat beside you."

"Yes," said Mr. Jones, "that seat is Mrs. Jones'."

"But couldn't Mrs. Jones come to the match?" said Joe.

"No she could not; Mrs. Jones died last week."

"I am sorry," said Joe, "but wouldn't one of your friends have liked Mrs. Jones' seat?"

"No," replied Mr. Jones, "my dear, loyal friends are all at Mrs. Jones' funeral today."

3 **A famous Olympic athlete has this to cite:**

From a schoolboy's essay on Johann Sebastian Bach: "Johann Sebastian Bach was a most prolific composer. He was the father of twenty children. In his spare time he practiced in the attic on a spinster."

4 An investment banker likes these two:

In an examination at Oxford, Oscar Wilde was required to translate from the Greek version of the New Testament, which was one of the set books. The passage chosen was from the story of the Passion. Wilde began to translate, easily and accurately. The examiners were satisfied, and told him that this was enough. Wilde ignored them and continued to translate. After another attempt the examiners at last succeeded in stopping him, and told him that they were satisfied with his translation.

"Oh, do let me go on," said Wilde, "I want to see how it ends."

"What's your idea of civilization?" Bernard Shaw was asked one day.

"It's a good idea," replied Shaw. "Somebody ought to start it."

5 Contributed by a professor verbatim from his three-year old grandson:

A little boy ate a lot of cup cakes as a snack. He asked for another, but his father said:

"If you eat another, you'll burst."

"Give me another and stand clear."

6 From an Air Vice-Marshal:

It was the end of the Battle of Britain. I had been summoned to a meeting at Fighter Command Headquarters. Approaching Stanmore by car I was stopped by a road sign which said, "Road Closed — Unexploded Bomb." There was a policeman on duty. I hailed him to find an alternative route. As he approached he was saying:

"Sorry. You can't go through, the bomb is likely to go off at any minute now."

On reaching my car he looked inside and noticing my uniform, stood back and said:

"I'm very sorry, sir. I didn't know you were a wing commander. It is quite all right for you to go through."

8

7 **A Professor of Astronomy and Geometry likes to tell this tale:**

There was a university in New England where the students operated a "bank" of term papers and other homework assignments. There were papers to suit all needs; it would look odd if an undistinguished student suddenly handed in a brilliant essay, so there were papers for an A grade, papers for a B and papers for a C. The papers guaranteed to get a safe and inconspicuous C were as popular as any.

In this university there was also a student who had spent the weekend on pursuits other than homework; so he went to the "bank." His course was a standard one, and the bank had several papers which had stood the test of time. He drew out a paper for a C, retyped it, and handed his work in.

In due course he received it back with comments in red ink and they went as follows:

"I wrote this paper myself twenty years ago. I always thought it should have had an A, and now I am glad to give it one."

8 **Four favorites of a Privy Councilman:**

A lost and exhausted climber was walking across a snow plateau when he suddenly became aware of a strong smell of fish and chips. Through the mist ahead he saw a Monastery and a priest and a monk standing in the doorway.

"You must be the Friar."

"No, he's the frier and I am the chip monk."

A man decides to spend a lazy weekend reading, goes to a bookshop and selects a book entitled "How to Hug." His disappointment can be imagined when he realized, when unwrapping it at home, that it was Volume VI of the Encyclopaedia Britannica.

Control to pilot: "What is your height and position?"
Pilot: "I'm 5 feet 8 and I'm sitting down."

A woman commissioned an artist to paint her portrait for a fee of $500. She immediately wrote out a check and handed it to him.
Artist: "I thought we had agreed to a fee of $500 but you have made out your check for $600."
Woman: "Yes, I know; but I find it a bit embarrassing. Would you have any objection to painting me in the nude?"
Artist: "None whatsoever provided I can keep my socks on as I must have somewhere to put my brushes."

9 **A Treasury official proffered this:**
There was this chap who had a great deal of trouble getting in touch with his firm of lawyers — a city firm with three partners, Smith, Brown & Robinson. Whenever he rang to speak to the partners they were unavailable. He would be told that "Mr. Smith was in the courts, Mr. Brown was on an overseas visit, and Mr. Robinson was tied up." Next time it was Mr. Smith who was abroad, Mr. Brown was in the courts, and Mr. Robinson was tied up!
This went on until eventually he expostulated:
"Look, I can understand that if a partner is out of the office, or abroad, I can't speak to him, but what about the partner who is in — how is it that Mr. Robinson always seems to be tied up?"
"Oh, you don't understand, sir. You see, whenever Mr. Smith and Mr. Brown have to be out of the office together, they always tie up Mr. Robinson!"

10 **The Ambassador to Luxembourg donated this:**
A nun who worked among children in the Middle East drove herself about her district by jeep, and was one day annoyed to find that not only had she run out of gas, but that the spare can she usually carried was missing from the vehicle. However, she remembered that she had passed a gas station a mile or so back, and being a woman of resource, she took out the only receptacle she had suitable for her purpose, a child's chamberpot,

trudged back to the garage, had the vessel filled, and trudged back to her stranded jeep.

When she unscrewed the gas tank cap and, with some difficulty, was pouring the contents of her pot into the tank, she became aware that an enormous Cadillac, full of wealthy oil sheiks, had stopped on the road beside her jeep, and the occupants were observing her with much interest. Eventually one of the Arabs got out and came over to her.

"Excuse me, Sister," he said courteously, "My friends and I would like to assure you that, although we obviously do not share your religion, we greatly admire your faith."

11 **A company director who served in Army remembers this:**

At camp the orderly officer of my regiment was on his rounds one day to find out whether there were any complaints. The men were having their midday meal and the officer said:

"Any complaints?"

"Yes, sir," said Private Thomson.

"Well!" said the officer, "what is your complaint?"

"Too much sand in the soup, sir," replied Private Thomson.

The officer said sternly:

"You have joined this regiment to serve your Country, understand."

"Yes, sir, to serve my Country but not to eat it."

12 **Preferred by a Treasury official:**

A vicar called on an old lady who was one of his parishioners and was very impressed by her talking parrot. But he noticed that the bird had a blue ribbon tied to each leg and asked the lady why.

"If I pull the ribbon on his right leg," she said, "he sings me a jolly hymn tune — Onward Christian Soldiers — but if I am in a sad mood, I pull the ribbon on his left leg and he suits my mood by singing — Abide With Me."

"Truly remarkable," said the vicar. "And what if you pull both ribbons at once?"

"Then I fall off my perch, you silly old fool," said the parrot.

13 Told by a member of the Security Commission:

A Yorkshire terrier and a Russian borzoi were waiting side by side outside a department store with their mistresses, and naturally fell into conversation.

"Have you always lived here?" asked the terrier.

"Oh no," said the borzoi, "I was brought up in Russia and in fact have spent most of my life there!"

"And what was life like over there?" asked the terrier.

"It was pretty good," said the borzoi, "I had a thermostatically heated kennel, mink-lined blankets and bones dipped in caviar (of which I am particularly fond)."

"Dear me," said the terrier, "Then why on earth did you come and live over here?"

"It's perfectly true that I don't have these comforts here," said the borzoi, "but the fact is, I do like to bark occasionally."

14 Three gems from a Rear-Admiral:

In my speech I will at least try and be brief —brevity exemplified in a certain Court when the convicted prisoner cried:

"As God is my Judge, my Lord, I am not guilty."

To which the Judge replied tersely:

"He's not, I am, you are, six months."

Those of you who speak Spanish, will, of course, know the old Castilian proverb that an after-dinner speech is like the horns of a bull — with a point here . . . and a point there . . . and an awful lot of bull in between . . . .

An old woman was sitting alone with her cat, polishing her lamp, when there was a sudden puff of smoke and a genii appeared and offered her three wishes. The old woman thought quickly and then said:

"I'd like to be rich, I'd like to be young again, and I'd like my cat to turn into a handsome prince."

Another puff of smoke and she found herself young and glamorous in a beautiful evening gown. The cat had disappeared but a gorgeous prince stood beside her, holding out his arms. As she melted into his embrace he murmured softly into her ear:

"Now I bet you're sorry you took me to the vet for that little operation."

15 From an old-time Civil Service Officer:

The Bishop was very thrilled by the fact that his wife had written a book; the fact that she had also presented him with a son ranked a poor second in his estimation. When a friend came up and shook him by the hand to congratulate him on his son and heir, he said:

"Congratulations, Bishop."

The Bishop replied:

"Thank you, I consider it a very estimable performance on the part of my wife considering that I gave her no assistance and she had very little help except from the minor canon."

16 A King Solomon is revealed by a Church Commissioner:

An English lady traveling in Germany left a valuable fur coat in charge of a German woman in the carriage. When she returned, the German was wearing the coat, and said that it belonged to her. The guard tried in vain to discover to which of the two it belonged, and finally sent them off to the Consul. The Consul asked to examine the coat, and brought it back a few moments later saying:

"This is a very serious affair; whoever the coat belongs to has been smuggling cocaine. Here are the two packets I found in the coat."

The German woman excused herself and bowed herself out of the room, saying:

"Just my little joke."

The English woman said:

"I can't understand how they could have got there."

The Consul replied:

"Don't worry, it is only salt, that I put there to find out whose coat it really was."

17 A Scottish landowner knows his geometry:

A mighty Indian chief had married three wives and allocated a wigwam to each of them. He promised that he would provide them with any sort of bed covering they wanted. The first and oldest, who was a well-brought-up and practical girl, asked for the hide of a buffalo, which was easily obtained. The second, who was intelligent but daring, asked for the pelt of a bear. This was a little harder and more dangerous for him but was nevertheless soon brought to her. The third wife was much the prettiest and most vivacious and she asked for the skin of a hippopotamus, which was a real challenge, but he finally succeeded in getting her one.

Nine months later the first wife had a boy, the second had a girl and the third had twins, a boy *and* a girl, which only goes to confirm that the squaw on the hippopotamus is always equal to the squaw on the other two hides.

18 The favorite dining-out story of a Solicitor-General:

At the annual dinner of the Central Borneo branch of a well-known organization, they were celebrating the end of the president's year of office.

Halfway through the second course, one member turned to his neighbor and said:

"I know I shouldn't say this, but I don't like our old president."

The neighbor replied cheerfully:

"Then just eat the vegetables."

19 A Logic Professor is expert on this subject:

It is related of Oscar Wilde that he was standing aloof at a party when his hostess came up to him and asked him anxiously:

"Are you enjoying yourself, Mr. Wilde?"

"Yes, I am," he said. "There is nothing else here to enjoy."

20 Charity begins at home, says this broadcasting official:

A Member of Parliament after a series of all-night sittings ran into trouble with his wife who doubted whether he spent all those hours in the House of Commons. On arriving home very early one morning he found a note left for him which read:

"The day before yesterday you came home yesterday morning,

yesterday you came home this morning, so if today you come home tomorrow morning, you will find that I left you yesterday."

Within a few hours of the death of a Congressman, a very eager prospective candidate telephoned the Speaker of the House:

"I was very sorry to hear of the death of Tom Atkins; is there any chance of me taking his place?"

The Speaker replied:

"Yes, if the undertaker has no objection."

21 **Short course in diplomacy from a Nigerian judge:**

When a diplomat says yes, he means perhaps; when he says perhaps, he means no; and if he says no, he is not a diplomat.

When a lady says no, she means perhaps; when she says perhaps, she means yes; and if she says yes, she is not a lady.

22 **From an Ambassador:**

Question: "How do you recognize a Scottish ship?"
Answer: "Because it is not followed by seagulls."

23 **True, says a Lord Mayor:**

Ad in South African paper:

"Lady who has cast off clothing of all descriptions invites inspection."

24 **Churchilliana from a Chancellor of the Exchequer:**

At a time when Winston Churchill was in the political wilderness, Bernard Shaw sent him four tickets for the first night of his new play, explaining in the covering letter that they were "for you and your friends — if you have any."

Churchill replied that he was returning the tickets because unfortunately he was busy on that evening, but would very much like to have tickets "for the second night — if there is one."

25 **A Bishop shows he is familiar with his parishioners:**

Two old sergeants were sitting in a shell hole on Anzio Beach during World War II in Italy. The shells were coming over thick and fast. One turned to the other and he said:

"Lofty, I'm scared stiff. Let's have a prayer."

"Prayer?" said the other, "What do you think this is, a Sunday school outing?"

Time passed by and the shells came still more thick and fast, bombs began to fall and all hell broke loose; whereupon the one turned to the other and he said:

"Lofty, I think we're in for it. Do you know any hymns?"

"Hymns?" said the other. "What do you think I am, an opera star?"

Ten more minutes went by and they thought that their last moment had come; whereupon the fellow took off his tin helmet, turned eyes to heaven and said:

"Lofty, I suggest that we do something religious — let's have a collection."

26 **Beloved tale of an industrialist:**

Scene: A supermarket.

Salesman (offering green peas in the pod).

Customer: "Gee! I've had them dried, frozen, packaged in cartons, and canned. Whatever will they think up next?"

27 A merry moment from a High Court Judge:

A man was feeling very peculiar — so peculiar that he sent for the doctor. The doctor came and gave him a thorough examination. At the end of it he said:

"I have some bad news and some good news. The bad news is that you are in for a change of sex."

"My God," said the man.

The doctor quickly intervened and said:

"Now for the good news; this will entitle you to play off the ladies' tees."

28 A favorite from a bank director:

The old clergyman was without doubt the world's worst golfer. One day, on a fairly long straight hole he uncorked a towering drive straight towards the pin. The ball started to roll and as if drawn by a magnet continued to roll — over the apron — across the green — hit the pin and dropped into the hole.

The astounded clergyman turned his eyes towards heaven.

"Lord," he begged, "I'd rather do it *myself*."

29 From the ex-president of the Liberal Party:

The late Noel Coward was taking one of his young godchildren for a walk when they saw two dogs mating.

"Oh, Uncle Noel, look at those dogs! What are they doing?"

"Well, one poor little doggie has gone blind and the other is pushing him all the way to the hospital."

30 This educational exposé comes from an engineer:

The visiting school inspector decided to take over a class which happened to be engaged on a Bible Study period. Selecting an encouraging looking boy in the front row, he said:

"Your name?"

"Smith, sir."

"Right, Smith. Now tell me, who blew down the walls of Jericho?"

"Please, sir, I didn't."

The inspector was angry at this cheeky answer and reported to the headmaster.

The headmaster said:

"Ah, Smith! Well, I happen to know Smith very well. He is a good and truthful boy, and you can take it from me that if he says he didn't do it then he certainly didn't do it."

The inspector was now even more incensed and duly reported the entire incident to the District Chief Education Officer.

The latter considered the situation and said:

"Well, in a case like this, I think we should take a broad view. Tell them to get an estimate for the repairs and I'll authorize it."

31 A Knight of the Garter has an ear for the garden:

Strawberries also have their little problems.

For example, one strawberry said to another on a certain sad occasion: "If we hadn't been in the same bed we wouldn't both be in this jam now."

32 How to outfox a bank, from a former Lord Mayor:

A wealthy man was advised by his bank manager that he had an overdraft of $100 and that interest would be charged at 12% per annum. The client insisted that he should deposit his Rolls-Royce car as security and drove it to the bank leaving it in the adjacent car park. A month later he returned to collect the car.

The curious bank manager asked him why he had insisted on depositing the car for security. The client with the overdraft replied:

"Where can you get car parking for a month for $1?"

33 Business is business, a Colonial Administrator proves:

An elderly man was lying in bed dying. He had obeyed all the commands of Jehovah, his life had been fruitful and his fortune had multiplied.

As his life ebbed away, his failing eyes told him that the family were gathered around the bed, but they were only hazy and indistinguishable forms. So he asked:

"Abraham, my boy, are you there?" "Yes, Father, I am here."

"Reuben, boy, are you there?"   "Yes, Father, I am here."

"Jacob, are you there?"   "Yes, Father, I am here."

"Rachel, are you there?"   "Yes, Father, I am here."

"Ephraim, are you there?"   "Yes, Father, I am here."

"Leah, dear, are you there?"   "Yes, Father, I am here."

"Esau, are you there?"   "Yes, Father, I am here."

"Moses, my son, are you there?"   "Yes, Father, I am here."

"Joseph, are you there?"   "Yes, Father, I am here."

"Sarah, my dear wife, are you there?" "Yes, yes, I am here."

The old man counted on his fingers, thought a moment, made an effort to sit up, and in great anxiety called out:

"Benjamin, are you here, too?"   "Yes, Father, I am here."

"Then who is looking after the business?" cried the old man with his last breath.

34 Two, with just the right touch from a businessman:

A shopkeeper noticed that a Scots customer was counting his change very carefully and seemed rather dubious about it.

"What's the matter, sir," he said, "your change is right, isn't it?"

"Aye," replied the Scotsman, "but it's only just right."

A golfer had a very dour Scots caddie. He was playing badly and, to hide his embarrassment, as he was about to take his fifth shot out of a bunker, he said to the caddie:

"Well, caddie, golf's a funny game, isn't it?"

"Aye," said the caddie, "but it's no meant to be."

35 Advice from an Employment Consultant:

If at first you don't succeed your successor will.

36 A Biochemistry Professor jibes at a colleague:

A physicist had a horseshoe hanging on the door of his laboratory. His colleagues were surprised and asked whether he believed it would bring luck to his experiments.

He answered:

"No, I don't believe in superstitions. But I have been told that it works even if you don't believe in it!"

37 An M.P. contributes domestic advice:

The most popular after-dinner speech on record was made by a man dining with his wife alone in the privacy of their home, and it consisted of one sentence containing seven words of one syllable:

"You leave them, dear, I'll do them."

38 A composer tells a story on himself:

One day I was rehearsing an orchestra, and I noticed one of the players had a nasty cough.

A glass of water was handed along to him, and I thought no more of it until I noticed quite a disturbance around him, and a good many smiles. I knew, but didn't, remember at the moment, that the gentleman concerned had a good thirst of his own, and I shouted out:

"What is the matter? Haven't you people ever seen a man drink a glass of water before?"

I chose my words badly: the answering chorus came back to me with superb ensemble:

"NOT THAT MAN!"

39 **An Irish politician provides a definition:**

The Perils of Logic:

The professor, wishing to establish a link between cause and effect, produced a flea to demonstrate his point. Placing the flea on the lectern he called on it to jump. And the flea jumped. Whereupon the great man produced a scalpel and cut off the flea's legs. The command "jump" was then repeated. And this time the flea remained stationary.

In triumph, the professor proclaimed to his students:

"My dear friends, we have now proved conclusively that when the legs of a flea are amputated the creature is rendered completely deaf!"

40 **A distinguished medical researcher on prunes:**

Andrew, a little boy aged 8, was the son of strict Presbyterian parents who doted on him. He was a very good little boy who did well both at day school and Sunday school, where he sang like a cherub. But one morning he apparently got out of bed on the wrong side, and came down to breakfast in a very cantankerous mood. At his place on the table was a plate of prunes.

"Andrew," said his mother, "you must eat your prunes."

"I don't want prunes," said Andrew.

"Andrew," said his mother in stern tones, "eat your prunes."

"I won't," said Andrew angrily.

"Andrew," said his mother, "you must not speak to your mother in that way. God has commanded little boys to honor their parents, and will punish those who do not." But Andrew was unmoved, and the prunes went back to the pantry uneaten.

Late that evening, after Andrew had gone to bed and while his parents were sitting by the fire downstairs, a thunderstorm blew up from the horizon. Gradually the lightning became more vivid and the thunder louder. In an interval between flashes, the parents heard Andrew's bedroom door open and footsteps come down the stairs and go into the pantry.

"Ah," said the delighted mother, "how wonderful. Now he has had his lesson."

At that moment there was an even more brilliant flash, and a deafening peal which shook the house. As the reverberations died away, Andrew's sweet little voice was heard coming from the pantry.

"Hell of a fuss about a few bloody prunes."

41 A sensible retort proferred by a Civil Aviation chairman:

Man leaving his home for a stag dinner, is challenged by his wife with the question.

"What would you do if you found me in bed with another man when you come back?"

He replied, without hesitation:

"Do? I would break his white stick, and shoot his seeing-eye dog."

42 A Chief of Air Staff cites an evasive trick:

During the war a man being medically examined for military service had to be rejected because all the tests the eye specialist applied seemed to indicate that the man was virtually blind.

The specialist felt that in some way he had been tricked and he was convinced of this when he called in at a local movie theater and found himself sitting next to the cause of his doubts. The specialist was looking around to find a military policeman to arrest the culprit, when the man put his hand on the specialist's arm and said:

"Excuse me, madam, can you tell me if this bus goes to California?"

43 A film producer offers this merry vignette:

A lady who lived in the country was invited to a wedding in London. One of her relations died and the funeral was fixed on the same day as the wedding and only an hour or two before the service. This placed her in rather a predicament as obviously the bright clothes which were suitable for a wedding would be unsuitable for a funeral and there was no time to change in between.

However, she decided to solve the problem by wearing a smart black suit for both occasions with a black hat for the funeral and to take a very gay flowered hat for the wedding. This she carried in a brown paper bag and, as she arrived only just before the funeral procession at the church, she hurriedly left it in the vestibule, so that she could pick it up again on her way out. She then went into the church and took her place in one of the pews.

A few minutes later when the coffin was carried up the aisle past her seat she was thunderstruck to see her best wedding hat placed on top of the coffin amongst the other floral tributes from the family. Later still, when the coffin was lowered into the grave, she had to stand by and see her treasured hat disappear forever into the depths of the earth.

44 **Short comment from a Marquess:**
Man in a pub: "Funny how my wife can spot blonde hairs, and miss garage doors."

45 **More truth than fiction from a Chief Rabbi:**
A refugee from the Nazis managed to get to Lisbon. He sought out the American Consul to try and obtain a visa to the United States. The Consul asked him where he had come from originally and he said Rumania. When asked whether he was a citizen of Rumania he replied in the affirmative, and the Consul said:

"I am sorry but the quota for immigrants from Rumania is already filled. You will have to wait for another eight years before your request can be considered."

As the refugee reached the door, he turned and asked the Consul:

"Will I have to come in the morning or in the afternoon?"

46 A Minister of Employment takes this out of his pocket:

Conjurer to yokel: "Now sir, would you be surprised if I took a rabbit out of your pocket?"

Yokel: "I would that."

Conjurer: "Why would you be surprised?"

Yokel: "Becos' I've got a ruddy ferret in it."

47 Two from a Stock Exchange member:

The Moderator of the General Assembly of the Church of Scotland was playing a round of golf with the Episcopal Bishop of Aberdeen. Nearing the 18th hole, their argument as to which of them was the more like God got steadily more heated. In the end they decided they would ask the first man they met to decide for them. As they approached the clubhouse a figure was seen to stagger down the steps and weave toward them.

"Come here, my man," said the Moderator. "His Lordship the Bishop and I wish you to listen to us and then decide which of us is the more like God."

"Oh," said the man, "that's easy, no bother at all, neither of you are, because I most clearly am. Just follow me and I'll prove it."

Whereupon he swung on his heels, followed by the astonished prelates, staggered up the steps, pushed his way through the door, turned straight into the bar. As the barman caught sight of his approach he said:

"Oh, God, not you again!"

A man staggered out of an auction parlor with a huge grandfather clock on his shoulder, turned right, heading up the street and knocked a frail old lady clean into the gutter.

She got up, dusted herself off and shouted at the man:

"You stupid idiot, why can't you wear a wrist watch like a civilized human being."

48 Culled from many a dinner attended by a football club director:

The after-dinner speaker went on and on until a guest was so fed up he picked up a bottle and aimed it at the speaker's head.

25

Unfortunately it hit a little man sitting beside him and this knocked him out. Immediately some of the people rushed to bring him around, and when eventually he came around, the only thing he was heard to say was:

"Please hit me again, I can still hear his voice."

49 **A true story:**

One day a friend of mine who had just been appointed head of a big mental establishment near London, asked me if I would like to be taken on a tour of the grounds. On the appointed day he met me at the big gates and as we walked towards the main building, a man carrying a suitcase was hurrying out. My friend said:

"I would like you to meet Patrick. He has just been discharged after 3 years here."

He called him over and said:

"Patrick, I would like you to meet the Colonel, who is Governor of the Tower of London and Keeper of the Crown Jewels."

Patrick gave me a long, queer look and then said:

"Don't you worry, old man. They will cure you too; when I came here I thought I was the Shah of Persia."

From the same man, the Governor of the Tower of London:

The local vicar had lost his bike and he told his attendant that on the following Sunday during his sermon he would bring in the Ten Commandments pausing significantly when he came to "Thou shalt not steal" while the attendant studied the faces of the congregation and tried to pick out the culprit. However, during the sermon, the vicar read through the Commandments without a pause.

After the service the attendant asked him why he did not pause, to which the vicar replied:

"When I got to 'Thou shalt not commit adultery', I realized where I had left my bike."

50 **Provided by a Member of the Industrial Court:**

A party of scientists from Russia recently visited England and the astronomers among them journeyed to the Royal Observatory at Herstmonceux.

They were shown the giant Isaac Newton telescope and one of them asked that it should be trained onto a particular portion of the sky. Looking through it and examining what he could see, he suddenly exclaimed:

"It is going to rain."

The Royal Observatory staff who were conducting the Russians around were astonished at this remark and wondered if the Russians had really discovered some means of telling the weather by examining a section of the sky through a telescope. They asked him how he could tell it was going to rain and the distinguished astronomer replied:

"My corns hurt."

51 **From the files of a Lord Justice:**

I was trying a divorce suit and when the wife petitioner was in the witness box I asked her:

"If your present marriage is dissolved would you like to marry again?"

She answered:

"No — but thank you very much."

52 **From a script writer who likes happy endings:**

An Englishman, a Frenchman and a Russian were trying to define true happiness.

"True happiness," said the Englishman, "is when you return home tired after work and find a gin and tonic waiting for you."

"You English have no romance," countered the Frenchman.

27

"True happiness is when you go on a business trip, find a pretty girl who entertains you, and then you part without regrets."

"You are both wrong," concluded the Russian. "Real true happiness is when you are home in bed at four o'clock in the morning and there is a hammering at the front door and there stand members of the Secret Police, who say to you, 'Ivan Ivanovitch, you are under arrest', and you are able to reply, 'Sorry! Ivan Ivanovitch lives next door'!"

53 **Good and brief from a TV performer:**
There is only one *ideal* after-dinner speech — and it consists of just five words:
"I will take the bill!"

54 **A businessman likes this bit of no-nonsense logic:**
An Englishman, a Frenchman and a German were arguing about the respective merits of their languages.

The Frenchman was saying that French was the language of love, the language of romance, the most beautiful and pure language in the world.

The German was asserting that German was the most vigorous language, the language of philosophers, the language of Goethe, the language most adaptable to the modern world of science and technology.

When the Englishman's turn came, he said:

"I don't understand what you fellows are talking about. Take this (and he held up a table knife). You in France call it un couteau. You Germans call it ein Messer. We in England simply call it a knife which, all said and done, is precisely what it is."

55 **Hear! Hear! from the Archbishop of Canterbury:**
The after-dinner speaker had been introduced in flattering terms. On rising to reply, he said:

"Such an introduction makes me pray two prayers for forgiveness: the first for my introducer, because he has told so many lies; second for myself, because I have enjoyed it so much."

28

56 From a Colonial Governor:

The wife of the Viceroy of India (to an aide at dinner party with music):

"Captain Mottram, do go and ask the bandmaster what is that charming tune!"

Aide (in full regimentals) marches to band, makes inquiry, returns, and stands to attention before the lady, clinking spurs:

"I shall remember your kisses, Your Excellency, when you have forgotten my name!"

57 Contributed by a Defence Minister:

The British Ambassador was in Washington some years back. About a fortnight before Christmas he was rung up by the local T.V. station.

"Ambassador," said the caller, "What would you like for Christmas?"

"I shouldn't dream of accepting anything."

"Seriously, we would like to know and don't be stuffy. You have after all been very kind to us during the year."

"Oh well, if you absolutely insist, I would like a small box of crystallized fruits."

He thought no more about it until Christmas Eve when he switched on the T.V.

"We have made a little Christmas survey all on our own," said the announcer. "We asked three visiting Ambassadors what they would like for Christmas.

"The French Ambassador said: 'Peace on earth, a great interest in human literature and understanding, and an end to war and strife.'

"Then we asked the German Ambassador and he said: 'A great upsurge in international trade, insuring growth and prosperity, particularly in the underdeveloped countries. That is what I wish for Christmas.'

"And then we asked the British Ambassador and he said he would like a small box of crystallized fruits."

58 **Offered by a Professor of Ornamental Design:**

A young man with expectations of inheriting from an aunt, discovered she was a lover of Keats. He therefore bought a mynah bird, taught it to recite "Ode to a Grecian Urn," and sent it off to his aunt.

After some weeks he rang to inquire whether his aunt had received the bird.

"Yes," she said, "and it was delicious."

Same contributor:

Two girls overheard on tube.

"I can't bear late nights. If I go out to dinner and am not in bed by twelve I go home."

59 **A ducky tale from a Police Commissioner:**

Having bought a gun dog and paid a good deal more for it than he had planned, or wished to pay, the dog's new owner was left with the uncomfortable and slightly guilty feeling which such circumstances inevitably provoke — that he had been less than sensible in his purchase, and perhaps even foolish. Nevertheless, being a keen wildfowler, it was not long before he visited a pond not far away from his home with the dog to try his luck with the morning flight. Not long after arriving there he was successful in shooting a duck which fell into the pond.

The new dog was told to fetch and straightaway ran over the surface of the water, picked up the floating body of the duck, returned with it running over the top of the water and laid it at the feet of the wildfowler.

As daylight strengthened so did the tally of ducks grow. All the birds fell into the pond when shot and all were retrieved by the dog running over the top of the water without even wetting its feet.

At the end of the shoot, and pondering on the dog's strange behavior as he walked around the edge of the pond in the direction of the place at which he had left his car, the wildfowler came upon a solitary fisherman engaged in putting up his rod, little stool, umbrella and all the other impedimenta which all fishermen seem to gather with such eagerness. He stopped to talk, and the two men were passing the time of day when a lone duck happened to come over. Quickly reloading, the wildfowler brought it down and the bird fell into the middle of the pond.

Once again, when commanded, the dog ran out over the top of the water, retrieved the duck, brought it back and laid it at his master's feet.

Neither wildfowler nor fisherman spoke. But as the former ejected the spent cartridge from his gun, put the duck into his bag and prepared to go on his way he said rather shamefaced:

"I only bought this dog a couple of days ago and, as a matter of fact, I foolishly paid a good deal more for it than I had intended and can afford."

There was silence and then the fisherman replied:

"Whoever persuaded you into that deal pulled a fast one on you; the dog can't even swim."

60 **A scientist offers these two:**

James Thurber tells of a teacher who gave her pupils a book on penguins to read and asked them to write an essay on it. My heart goes out to the little girl whose essay consisted of a single sentence.

"This book," she wrote, "told me more about penguins than I wanted to know."

Will, aged seven years, had something of a reputation at school for not paying attention. He came home one day and proudly announced to his mother that the class had had a lecture from a visitor.

"What was it about?" asked his mother.

"I don't know," came the reply.

"Why, weren't you listening?"

Will was outraged.

"Of course I was listening," he said indignantly. "The man didn't tell us what it was about."

I believe I have heard that lecture, too.

61 **From a Member of the House of Lords:**

A little group of us were standing talking in a corridor of the House of Lords, when along came an old hereditary Peer who had recently married a young wife. We congratulated him. He thanked us and said:

"I must have an heir; I must have an heir."

As he tottered off down the corridor one of the group said:

"The old boy is certainly heir minded but I doubt if he's heir conditioned."

62 **A modest story from a Viscount:**

An Irishman from County Tyrone invited to a shoot in England was given a place next to his host who took the end of the line.

The cry of "mark over" was followed by the sight of a cock pheasant flying directly along the line. Each gun in turn missed and in taking evasive action the old pheasant was at quite a height by the time it came over the Irishman, whose shot brought the bird down with a tremendous crash.

"Oh! good shot, Murphy," called his host, "a remarkable shot."

To which his guest modestly replied:

"Sure it was nothing at all; the fall would have killed him anyway."

63 **From the repertoire of a noble landowner and farmer:**

The cannibal's wife went to the cannibal butcher and said she wanted to give her husband a treat for the Sunday lunch.

"What," said the butcher "does he like?"

"He is particularly fond of brains. What have you?"

"We have Missionary's Brains at 30¢ a lb."

"I think we had that last time," said the wife.

"Well, we have Seaman's Brains at 35¢ a lb."

"I hear they are rather salty: have you any more?"

"Yes, we have Governors' Brains; but they are 90¢ a lb."

"This is scandalous," said the housewife. "30¢ and 35¢ yes, but 90¢ is ridiculous. I shall report you to the Prices and Incomes Board."

"Please, madam, don't," said the butcher. "You've no idea the number of Governors we had to kill to get a pound's worth of brains."

64 **The favorite retort of a titled solicitor:**

My uncle, a country parson and a connoisseur of port, went to dine one night with his rural dean. The rural dean, though rich, was notorious for the inferior wines that he used to produce for visiting clergy. After dinner my uncle sniffed the port suspiciously and gingerly sipped it. A look of surprise came over his face and turning to his host he exclaimed:

"Henry, this is Cockburn 1908! Where on earth did you get it?"

To which the rural dean replied:

"My dear Alec, on the rare occasion when you produce a good sermon I don't ask you where you got it from."

65 **Saying from a Lord Mayor:**

Rejoinder to bombastic cleric interrupting a speaker:

"If the meek shall inherit the earth, you are bankrupt right now."

66 **Note from a Musical Director:**

Two Irishmen were working on a building site. The first Irishman, Pat, shouts to his companion, Mick:

"Hey, watch out, Mick, the bricks are falling out of the wall."

Just then, a brick falls and hits Mick, taking off his ear. Mick falls to the ground bleeding profusely but Pat says:

"Take it easy, Mick, I'll find your ear and we'll take you to hospital, they'll soon sew it back on."

Pat searches among the rubble, finds Mick's ear and takes it over to where Mick is lying.

"O.K.," says Pat, "I've got it."

Mick looks at it:

"That's not mine, you bloody fool — mine had a cigarette behind it."

67 Story from a Mayor's mixed bag:

Three Cambridge dons were walking by the river one beautiful hot summer day, and coming to a secluded spot could not resist the temptation to have a dip. Not having costumes with them they went in "in the buff." Unfortunately, just as they came out, a boat full of pretty female undergrads came around the bend, whereupon in some consternation two of the dons grabbed some clothes around their middles, while the third threw something over his head!

After the girls had gone, the two who had covered their middles turned on the other and said:

"Why on earth did you do that?"

Whereupon he answered:

"Where I come from we recognize people by their faces!"

68 An Air Vice-Marshal tells three true stories:

A distinguished French politician having celebrated his 90th birthday was asked by a friend:

"How do you find life now you are 90?"

"Fine, when you consider the alternative."

A Member of Parliament in an after-dinner speech went on for an incredibly long time. When he finally sat down he said to his neighbor:

"How did that go?"

After thought, the neighbor replied:

"At least it will shorten this ruddy winter."

An old man was asked by a friend:

"What do you do now that you have retired?"

He replied:

"My man brings me a cup of tea in the morning and a copy of 'The Times.' I drink the tea and read the obituaries and if I am not included therein I get up out of bed."

69 A Lieutenant-General's contribution:

Two young men were on a walking tour in Wales. They stayed one night at a lonely house, where they were offered a room each by the owner, a middle-aged woman living alone who was clearly doing her best to conceal her age.

Next morning they left after paying their bill.

Nine months later one of them received a solicitor's letter, which surprised him. He rang up his friend and the following conversation ensued:

"Do you remember the house we stayed in during our walking tour in Wales last year, where there was a blousy looking woman living alone?"

"Yes, I remember her well."

"Did you leave your room during the night and visit her room?"

"Yes, as a matter of fact, I did."

"Did you, by any chance, give her my name instead of yours?"

"Yes, I'm sorry about it, and I should have told you before — I hope nothing has gone wrong."

"That explains it. Today I received a solicitor's letter saying that she had died, and left me £10,000 in her will."

70 Donated by a barrister:

Two elderly sisters were most devout and regular attenders at the church every Sunday morning. The minister was a fine God-fearing man whose only fault, if it is a fault, was that his sermons were never less than fifty minutes.

On one particular Sunday he excelled himself by continuing for over an hour, and was still going strong, when one of the sisters (very deaf) turned to the other and asked in a loud voice:

"Is he no feenished yet?"

To which the other replied:

"Aye, he's feenished, but he canna stop!"

71 From a Lord Lieutenant:

At a crowded dinner party:

"Can you all hear me at the back of the room?"

A voice from the back of the room:

"Yes, I can hear you perfectly well, but I don't mind a bit changing with somebody who can't."

72 A diplomat's favorite:

The head of a College was in the hospital for some time. The governing body met in his absence and decided to send him a telegram.

It read: "Governing body met today, and wish you a speedy recovery by 18 votes to 17."

73 A Vice-Admiral likes this one:

The other morning in our pasture, I heard two of our cows talking.

One said to the other:

"Daisy, you're not looking very well this morning, are you feeling all right?"

Daisy replied:

"No, I'm not — in fact I'm feeling awful. The trouble is that I went to several parties last night — the first was with the Guernseys, then on to the Herefords and finishing with the Aberdeen Angus. Anyhow, I didn't wake up this morning, I missed being milked — and now I've got a hell of a hang-under."

74 A distinguished English Professor shares a classic puzzler:

A New York gentleman buttered a piece of toast during breakfast, then accidentally dropped it on the floor. He bent down to pick it up, and saw to his astonishment that it had landed butter side up, which he knew from experience was against all the laws of nature. Buttered bread or toast always fell butter side down. He was so puzzled by what happened that he went to see his rabbi to whom he explained what had happened.

"How can you explain such an astonishing and unnatural event?" he asked.

The rabbi pondered a while, then told the gentleman he would have to consult various authorities before he could give a definite reply. So would the gentleman please come back in a week's time.

The following week the gentleman returned.

"Well, rabbi," he said, "have you found the explanation of that extraordinary matter of the buttered toast?"

"Well," the rabbi replied, "I have consulted many books and talked with many colleagues. It seems that there is only one possible explanation. You must have buttered the toast on the wrong side."

75 **A Musical Director enjoys this anecdote:**

Pierre Monteux, the famous conductor, was reputed to have been interviewed on television on his 90th birthday. Asked what his pleasures in life were at the age of 90, this alert Frenchman replied:

"I still have two abiding passions; one is my model railway, the other — women. But — at the age of 90, I find I am getting just a little too old for model railways."

76 **A Parliamentarian presents this argument:**

A doctor, an architect and a politician argued as to whose was the oldest profession.

"Obviously, the medical profession is the oldest," said the doctor, "since the first doctor was the one who took the rib out of Adam to create Eve."

The architect disagreed.

"The first architect created order out of chaos in the firmament, so mine must be the oldest profession."

"Ah!" said the politician, "but it was the first politician who created the chaos."

77 **Shared by a Colonial:**

"What kind of shot is our distinguished guest?" Lord Minto, one-time Viceroy of India, asked the native bearer, who had attended an American guest.

"Oh," replied the Indian, "the young sahib shot divinely but Allah was merciful to the birds."

78 A film executive is fond of this one:

The scene is a monastery where every seven years a monk is selected to pass an opinion of life within the community.

At one of the seven-year meetings, the Abbot calls upon Brother Albert to say what he feels, and the privileged monk asks:

"Why is our soup always cold?"

Seven years later, Brother John is invited to speak, and he says:

"The soup is not always cold but is sometimes hot."

Another seven years pass and this time Brother Richard is called upon. He says:

"I want to resign the Order."

When asked why, he contends:

"I'm sick and tired of this constant bickering."

79 Thanks to a Lord Mayor of London for this:

A nonconformist minister who had preached vigorously all his life against the wickedness of betting found himself in Ireland and was tempted to attend a race meeting, to see for himself what went on. Not surprisingly he saw one Catholic priest, if not more, there and he actually saw one bless a horse about to run in a race.

He remembered the number of the horse, which won the race. His curiosity roused further, he continued to watch the priest, whom he saw bless, respectively, two more horses who also won their races.

By then, completely demoralized, the minister convinced himself that there was no chance about the outcome and, after seeing a horse for the fourth race being blessed, he hastily placed all his money upon it. The race started but before very long the horse began to falter and finally dropped down dead.

Distraught, the minister sought out the priest and told him his unhappy experience.

The Catholic was distressed and said: "You must be a Protestant!"

"Indeed I am," said the nonconformist.

The other replied: "Sure then you would not be knowing the difference between a blessing and giving the last rites!!"

80 **A Duke's donation:**

I was sitting next to a very distinguished man at a large public dinner at which I was about to speak; my neighbor was not on the list of speakers, and I turned to him and said:

"Oh how I hate having to make a speech."

To which he replied, fixing me with steely look:

"Oh do you, I don't mind a bit, I just can't bear listening."

81 **Two celebrity stories from a Member of the European Parliament:**

Sam Goldwyn, when being reminded that "You can't take it with you," replied: "Then I will not go."

Groucho Marx taking Harpo's pulse and remarking:

"Either he is dead or my watch has stopped."

82 **The choice of a broadcaster's collection:**

An American is on his first visit to Scotland.

At breakfast he finds his host seated before a plate of porridge. He watches fascinated; then asks:

"Are you going to *have* that?"

There is a pregnant pause and then the American is struck by an awful thought. He adds in awesome tones:

"Or have you *had* it?"

83 **From a judge's point of view:**

Greater love hath no man than this — that he giveth away his best after-dinner story to charity:

A schoolmaster who tried to teach me divinity went on a trip to the Holy Land, and took a boat on the Sea of Galilee for which he was in his view overcharged. He paid . . . and, as an afterthought, gently remarked:

"No wonder Jesus walked."

84 Courtesy of a radio and television executive:

A small and weedy man arrived at a lumberjack camp in the northern forests of Canada. As all the men working at the lumberjack camp were at least six feet tall and big husky men at that, they simply couldn't believe that the new arrival was in fact a lumberjack. They therefore gave him a very small axe and took him to a small sapling. The man duly spat on each palm and with two flicks of his wrists chopped the sapling down.

The big husky lumberjacks immediately thought that he was making fun of them and so decided to teach him a lesson. They gave him one of the largest and heaviest axes that they could find and took him to a particularly tall and thick tree.

"Go on, cut this down," they said.

"All right," he replied.

Again he spat on his palms, picked up the axe and was just about to hit the tree when he turned to them and said: "But you have not given me the line."

Whereupon the lumberjacks thought, "He evidently does know a bit about it," and so they pointed to another tall tree on the horizon.

Within a very few minutes the new arrival had sent the big tree crashing down absolutely straight on the line given.

"Amazing," said the lumberjacks, "but how on earth is it that someone as small and weedy looking as you are can fell trees so well; where exactly do you come from?"

"The Sahara," he replied.

"But there are no trees in the Sahara," said one of the lumberjacks.

"Not any more," replied the new arrival.

85 **Offering from a Bishop:**

A young ordinand, who was being sent as curate to a country parish, was worried by his lack of experience in country matters. He therefore decided that perhaps he could make a start by teaching himself how to milk a cow.

Seizing a bucket and stool, he approached a likely looking cow in the middle of a field and set to work. The cow had other ideas, and moved off across the field; whereupon the young man picked up his bucket and stool and started again. Once more the cow moved off and the young man with it.

When this had happened several times, a friend who was watching from the road shouted to the ordinand:

"What are you doing?"

Back came the reply:

"About three miles to the gallon."

86 **A goldsmith values this story:**

I was asked to present the prizes at a girls' school. It is always difficult to think of something to say other than, "Congratulations," "Well done," etc.

The girls came up in age groups and eventually the head girl came up to collect the several prizes she had won. She was a nice looking girl of about 17. I wondered what I could say to her. Suddenly I thought that as this was her last term it would be appropriate to ask her:

"And what are you going to do when you leave school?"

She looked at me very coyly and said:

"Well, I *had* thought of going straight home."

87 **A thought to ponder, from a government official:**

A British diplomat was asking Mao Tse-tung some questions after having been granted a rare interview.

"What do you think would have happened if Mr. Khrushchev had been assassinated instead of President Kennedy?"

Chairman Mao thought and then said:

"I don't think Mr. Onassis would have married Mrs. Khrushchev."

88 **Joke from an Army man:**

How do elephants make love under water?

They first remove their trunks.

89 **A judge likes this classic:**

An Anglican vicar noticed that an Evangelical neighbor was having some success with posters displaying slogans exhorting this and that, and decided to follow suit.

After much thought he devised a winner:

"IF YOU'RE TIRED OF SIN STEP IN."

Imagine the poor man's chagrin when the next day he saw this written below his text:

"BUT IF YOU ARE NOT, PHONE JUDSON 6-8999.

90 **An Air Marshal is keen on this water story:**

Scene: The small mail steamer from Glasgow on its route up the West coast of Scotland.

On the bridge the captain and a couple of lady schoolteachers he had invited up there.

A heavy shower of rain approaches. Captain in a loud voice

down the "voice-pipe"
to the saloon below
where one of his crew
is in charge of the bar:

"Is there a big
mackintosh down there
that would cover two
ladies?"

Reply, by a small
man in the corner,
after a moment's
silence:

"Noo, but there is a
wee MacGregor here
that is prepared to try."

91 **The head of the Entertainers' Association is amused by this:**

Two Scottish sailors were going home on leave after a rough
time in the undeclared Cod War between Iceland and Great
Britain. Arriving at their home port to go on their leave they got
into a train and found themselves sharing a compartment with a
parson.

After the train moved off a little, one sailor says to the other:

"What are you going to do with your leave, Jack?"

"I am going to get drunk on beer every night. That's my hobby.
How about you?"

The other sailor says:

"Girls are my hobby. I am going to see a different one every
night and have a marvelous time."

The train moves on. One sailor looks at the paper and on
reading it says to his friend:

"What's lumbago, Jack?"

"I don't know — ask the parson," was the reply.

So the sailor says:

"What's lumbago, sir?"

As the parson was annoyed at the way they had been talking,
he replied:

"Lumbago, my man, is a very painful disease, due to drinking beer and going out with women. Why do you ask?"

"It's nothing, guv'nor — it just says in the paper here that the Bishop of London has got it."

92 **From Russia with love—from an industrialist:**

Here is a true story about a visit to Russia, and the moral is always take your own interpreter — because the official one provided will almost certainly give a somewhat watered-down version of what was actually said.

We were visiting metal factories and were accompanied by a Mr. B., from the ministry concerned.

One factory manager, in the course of polite small-talk, said:

"Mr. B. who is with you is a very eminent metallurgist in our country. A few years ago he won the Stalin Prize for Metallurgy."

Mr. B. then replied in Russian and we got two nearly simultaneous translations.

The local guide said:

"Mr. B. said that because he won the Stalin Prize, he had had no unfair promotion."

Our interpreter than chipped in to say that what he had really said was:

"And a fat lot of bloody good that did me!"

93 **The former Governor of Northern Ireland recalls this chuckler:**

The air-raid warden on his rounds in a populous and dark area of Glasgow observed a light which he went to investigate. The following conversation took place between him and a small boy who answered his knock on the door.

Warden: "Is your father in?"

Boy: "No, my father went oot when my mither came in."

Warden: "Is your mother in?"

Boy: "No, my mither went oot when my brither came in."

Warden: "Is your brother in?"

Boy: "No, my brither went oot when I came in."

Warden: "Then are you in charge of the house?"

Boy: "It's no a hoose, it's a lavatory!"

A certain organization required a replacement for one of their top officials who was shortly to reach the age of retirement. The post, a highly paid one, called for exceptional qualifications and accordingly an advertisement, setting out the conditions, was inserted in the press.

Sometime later the board met to consider the applications and to prepare a short list for interviews, and among the applicants appeared the name of a Mr. A. His age and his qualifications exactly fitted the company's requirements and the chairman was delighted. In fact, he suggested that they need hardly look further.

However, one of the members interrupted and said:

"I do not know Mr. A. personally but I have heard that he is inclined to lift his elbow to a startling degree and I feel we should proceed with caution."

Following some discussion and in view of A's high qualifications, it was decided to continue to consider him and at the same time to find out whether his drinking habits were as bad as they were alleged to be. So, on the appointed day when those left on the list were assembled and Mr. A. was ushered into the board room, the chairman opened by saying:

"Good morning, Mr. A. Please sit down. Do smoke if you wish."

There followed a series of technical questions on the conclusion of which, the chairman said:

"Now, Mr. A., the board would like to ask you certain questions of a different nature and the first is — supposing the word 'Haig' was mentioned to you, what would it remind you of?"

Without hesitation Mr. A. replied:

"I would immediately recall that famous Commander-in-Chief, Earl Haig, who led the British Forces to victory in France, in the First World War."

"Thank you," remarked the chairman. "But supposing I said 'White Horse' — what then?"

"Ah," retorted Mr. A., "I would remember the pleasant days I have spent in the Vale of the White Horse in the beautiful English countryside in spring and summer."

"Now, one last question," continued the chairman, "What are your immediate reactions to the words 'VAT 69'?"

Mr. A. looked puzzled and, after a moment's thought, replied:

"Gentlemen, I fear you have me beaten there. Could it possibly be the Pope's telephone number?"

95 A Major-General's favorite:

A friend once introduced me as "This Battle-Scared Warrior."

Realizing his mistake, he hastily corrected himself: "I . . . I . . . mean This Bottle-Scarred Warrior!"

And another from the same contributor:

The missionary met a man-eating lion in the bush. He fell on his knees and buried his face in his hands. Peeping through his fingers, he saw the man-eater on its knees in front of him, paws in eyes.

Unable to bear it longer, the missionary shouted:

"I'm praying to be delivered from the jaws of the lion. What on earth are you doing?"

The lion growled back: "I'm saying grace!"

96 Offered by Glasgow's Town Clerk:

The local Health Officer was investigating a report about vibration being felt on the floor of a high-rise apartment house. His first reaction was that there was no evidence to support the complaint. The woman of the house explained, however, that the trouble was at its worst when she was lying in bed and a double-decker bus passed. She invited the inspector to lie on the bed and experience the vibration for himself.

No sooner had he done so than the husband came in. The inspector's embarrassment prompted the immediate explanation: "I doubt if you are going to believe me, mister, but I'm just waiting for a bus."

97 From a Trade Union Secretary:

A big local authority in the North of England had received a bequest of a large estate including a mansion house and a lake. The council had already decided that the mansion would be a museum and art gallery and the lake would be a pleasure area and have a boathouse.

An independent councillor moved that the council should purchase a gondola for the lake. A member of the ruling party immediately moved an amendment that they should buy two, breed from them and sell the progeny to other authorities and thus be self-supporting.

The Lord Mayor, appalled at the ignorance of his colleagues, said:

"Please withdraw your amendment — don't you know that a gondola is a cheese!"

98 As told by a company chairman in India:

A friend of mine was traveling in a train and opposite him sat a gentleman reading "The Times." Every now and then he took a complete sheet of the newspaper, crumpled it up, opened the window, threw it out and shut the window.

After he had done this two or three times my friend said:

"Excuse me, sir, but I am most interested in what you are doing. May I ask why you do it?"

"Oh yes," he replied, "it keeps the elephants away."

"But," my friend said, "there aren't any elephants here."

"Of course not," came the answer. "That proves it works!"

99 A Professor of Statistics gives us this incident:

Some years ago, I took my two younger children to an evening for children at the Harvard University Observatory. Of course the sky was cloudy, and except for a brief glimpse of the moon the telescopes could give no satisfaction. We were then assembled in a lecture room, perhaps 200 in all — more than half children, and these mostly under 10 and all looking highly intelligent. A young astronomer gave an excellent talk on "The Sizes of Heavenly Bodies," well illustrated with the aid of an enormous balloon. Around me I could see notes being made by tiny hands with small pencils and scraps of paper.

After about 40 minutes, the lecturer stopped and rashly invited questions.

Behind me a little 7-year-old voice piped up; reading from his carefully prepared paper, he asked — with a clarity that could well be imitated by older questioners at scientific or political meetings:

"Will the lecturer please tell us how far it is from the Earth to the planet Mercury?"

The lecturer was a cautious scientist, unwilling to risk an approximate truth.

"It depends," he said, "on the time."

Back came the small boy: "Well, say at 6:30."

100 **A Viscount recounts:**

When asked which piece of the salmon he would prefer, the local farmer replied:

"The tail end, starting from just behind the ears."

101 **A revealing anecdote from a Parliamentarian:**

The old lady was dying. Her husband was by her bedside. Her chief joy in life had been cooking him a good breakfast each morning.

"When I am gone, John," she said, "you will marry again soon, won't you, so that you can get a good breakfast in the mornings."

"My dear," said her husband, "don't talk of such things. I am not thinking of marrying again."

"But, John, I won't go happy unless you find another wife soon. She can have everything of mine except my clothes. Remember that John, not my clothes."

"It's all right, my dear," said John, "they wouldn't fit her."

102 **An author and Ambassador likes this tale:**

An Ambassador once traveled from Paris to Istanbul on the Orient Express, and was bitten by bugs on the way. He sent a strong complaint to the railway company, and in reply received a letter stating that they were horrified that so eminent a person should have suffered in this way; that such a thing had never in their experience happened before; that they were taking stringent measures to prevent any possibility of a recurrence; and that they begged him to accept their humblest apologies.

All very proper. But unhappily the clerk who dealt with the complaint, by inadvertence, attached to this reply the Ambassador's original letter of complaint, across which someone had scribbled:

"Usual bug letter please."

103 **Reaction analysis by an Air Vice-Marshal:**

The really significant difference between the various nationalities is the way they react to a funny story.

When you tell an Englishman a funny story he laughs three times — the first time when you tell it to him, the second time when you explain it to him, and the third time when he catches on.

A Russian on the other hand only laughs twice — the first time when you tell it to him, the second time when you explain it to him — he never catches on.

A German will laugh just once because he catches on straight away.

And an American doesn't laugh at all because he's heard it before.

104 **A clever classic from a College Registrar:**

Four old English gentlemen made it a practice to walk across the city park in the long summer evenings, chatting of art, literature and music. They were the Leader of the City Silver Band, the City Librarian, the City Baker and a very old and revered Professor of English.

They all enjoyed these excursions, and were so engaged one long summer evening when they came across four young ladies of obvious easy virtue sitting on a park bench; the four young ladies wished the old gentlemen "Good evening," and wondered if they might be of service. Graciously the old gentlemen refused the offer and continued their walk in deep thought.

After a while a voice said:

"Do you know, I've never seen *four* of those together before, I've seen them singly, of course, but one wonders, what would be the collective noun for a body such as that?"

The City Baker thought that the collective noun was a JAM of tarts.

The Leader of the City Silver Band inclined toward a FLOURISH of strumpets.

After much thought the City Librarian said that they were a VOLUME — of trollops.

The old Professor of English, however, walked on ahead shaking his white mane.

"You are all quite wrong, quite wrong. They are neither a *Jam*, nor a *Flourish* nor a *Volume*."

"What then, Professor?"

"Undoubtedly the collective noun for a group such as that would be an ANTHOLOGY."

"An anthology, Professor?"

"Yes. An Anthology of English Prose."

105 **A Lord High Chancellor reminisces:**

I was sorry for the man in the dock at the Court. He was a "con" man and he had gone to some trouble, in a period of imprisonment, to think out his next get-rich-quick scheme. He eventually acquired a small bookshop from which he made a very modest income. He became, however, very well-to-do because he read the obituaries in "The Times" and whenever a clergyman died he sent in a bill marked "To Account Rendered" for $50.35, or some modest amount. (It is extraordinary how many clergymen die.)

Almost inevitably he received a check in settlement. Sometimes if the executor was a difficult lawyer or accountant he wrote and asked for a copy of the account. He would then be sent a copy of the full account containing "The Sexual Life of Greece and Rome," "Lady Chatterley's Lover," etc., and then he paid very quickly.

After a few years he had some very bad luck; the attorney for the executors was a tiresome man and brought the bookdealer up short. The deceased had been blind for nine years.

106 **Told by an Ambassador:**

A poor old widow woman in Australia was one day invited to come to a lawyer's office to be told that a distant relative in England had died and left her a lot of money. The dear old thing was quite overcome; what was she going to do with all that money at her age?

"Well," suggested the lawyer, "what about making a trip to England to see the old country for yourself?"

"What, me?" said the old woman. "Me go to that country where all those convicts came from?"

107 Passed along by a newspaper executive:

In the Senior Common Room, the members of an Oxford College were considering what to invest some college funds in.

The Bursar recommended land.

"Land," he said, "has proved a very good investment for the last one thousand years."

There was a murmur of approval from his colleagues except for the history don.

"That's all very well," said he, "but you must remember the last thousand years have been quite exceptional."

108 A retired wine merchant pours this one out:

An English golfer playing at Muirfield for the first time with a very dour Scottish caddie arrived at the third hole and after a good drive asked his caddie what club to take.

"You'll be wanting your spoon," was the laconic reply.

"I don't like the lie much," said the Englishman, "I think I'll try my 3 iron."

He was handed it without a word and made a wonderful shot pitching just short of the green and then running into the hole.

"How about that?" he said, turning to the caddie.

"Aye, it was a good shot but ye'd have done better with yer spoon."

109 A slice of life from a Professor of Surgery:

Jock McTavish couldn't sleep. He twisted and turned so much that his wife Jean asked him what was the matter.

"Ah'm worried," he said. "You see, six months ago I borrowed £50 from Angus McFlannel across the road, and I cannot pay it back. Ah've no idea how I'll raise the money, and I'm so worried about it."

On hearing this, Jean got promptly out of bed, went over to the window, opened it wide and yelled across the street:

"Hey, Maggie — Maggie McFlannel!"

Eventually a sleepy female head in curlers appeared at a window directly opposite and yelled back:

"What is it?"

Jean went on:

"My Jock owes your Angus £50 and he canna pay it back."

Whereupon she slammed the window shut again, got back into bed, turned to her husband and said:

"There's no need for you to worry any more. Now he's worrying about it. Get back to sleep."

110 **A landowner furnished this:**

A young man bought a new fast car and tried it out on a nearly straight road in Ireland where he lived.

He accelerated to 60, 70, 80, and realized the straight yet narrow road went over a hilltop. But there was never any traffic so he topped the rise at 100. Standing on the road talking were two Irishmen with a tractor alongside, completely blocking the way. The car swerved to the left, went over the fence, across the field, through the next fence and shuddered to a halt.

One Irishman turned to the other and said:

"Begorrahh, Paddy, we just got out of that field in time."

DANGER
LOW FLYING
CARS

111 **From a Bishop:**

A Very Important Person was aggravated by what he considered to be incompetent service from the new steward at his club.

"Do you know who I am?" he thundered.

"No, sir," was the reply, "but I will make inquiries and then come and tell you."

112 **A gem from a Maritime Consultant:**

The master of a ship was observed, each time she put to sea, to go to the safe, unlock it, extract a large black book, read carefully, replace it in the safe and lock it up.

The other officers were most curious but could never get hold of the old man's keys.

One day the master died and was buried at sea in the customary way, but the chief officer had taken care to get hold of the keys.

Eagerly the safe was unlocked, the book extracted and opened.

There was a single entry:

"Port is on the left, starboard on the right."

113 **Thanks for this to the Queen's Mother's Comptroller:**

An after-dinner speaker as he was ending his speech said:

"And now I feel like Lady Godiva, who as she approached the end of her ride through Coventry said to herself — thank goodness I'm nearing my close."

114 **Our gratitude to the High Sheriff of Nottingham:**

On a long wartime rail journey in the U.K., a G.I. took a 1st class ticket, only to find all seats taken, forcing him to stand in the corridor.

On walking along the train, he found a dog sitting on one seat. Inquiry to its lady owner simply produced:

"I have paid for Fifi's ticket, so Fifi sits in a seat."

At intervals, this same conversation is repeated, until the G.I. was so infuriated he seized the dog and threw it out of the window. Whereupon one of the other U.K. passengers remarked:

"You Americans do everything wrong; you drive on the right; you eat dinner at 6 p.m.; you think we British despise you; and now you've thrown the wrong bitch out of the window."

115 From the former Head of the Diplomatic Service:

Once upon a time, a quarter of a century ago, there lived in Washington, D.C., a newspaper columnist called George Dixon. To be met with in any choice bar, he had a round (not fat) body, close-cropped hair, a round face, round horn-rimmed glasses and a hearty greeting for everybody. This was combined with a profound mistrust of all people of intellectual or social pretensions, like Democratic politicians or Britishers generally. Here is one of his anecdotes, not, regrettably, in his own words except for the last line which is genuine.

At a marble-topped table in an old-fashioned café there sat a somewhat gloomy man sipping intermittently from a glass. There were other such tables around, one very much in a corner.

Looking up from his glass, the gloomy man pointed to the corner table and said firmly: "Waiter, there's a pigeon under that table."

"But, sir, this restaurant is fully screened, every precaution is taken . . ."

"There is a pigeon under that table."

After more such argument, the waiter and a colleague dragged away the heavy table with difficulty from the corner.

"Yes, sir," said the pigeon, "any messages?"

116 A Navy Captain remembers:

A young mother (let us call her "Susan") was as most mothers are, inordinately proud of her first baby, so when Susan's mother came to stay she suggested that the old lady might like to see baby have its bath. Having done so, Susan asked her mother what she thought of the baby.

"Oh, I think it's a splendid child," she replied, "but tell me is it a boy or a girl?"

"Have you lost or mislaid your spectacles?" said Susan.

"No, darling, but I've lost my memory!"

117 A computer joke from a Minister of Housing:

A parliamentary candidate was touring an office which was computerized. He suggested that they should ask the machine what the result of the election would be. Back came the reply:

"It says that *you* will win, but that personally it would not vote for you."

118 An actor wants us to know:

This report appeared in "The Shetland Times" many years ago. This newspaper, still going strong, was co-founded by my grandfather just over 100 years ago.

"During the funeral procession of Mr. William Johnson, who died at the age of 79, his boyhood friend John Jamieson, aged 77, dropped dead at the graveside. Naturally this threw a gloom over the entire proceedings."

119 From a Member of the House of Lords:

After riding a gallop on my horse, one of the trainer's grooms came in on foot and stated:

"I am terribly sorry, he fell dead. He has never done that before."

120 From a missionary's collection:

My best after-dinner story was provided 50 years ago by an old Amazonian Indian (Amerindian). After a forest feast, when they had discussed whether to kill me, he said (I translate):

"I am not in favor; the last time we killed a white man, not a mouthful was given to me."

121 A College Principal on Bowdlerizing:

There is, after all, something to be said for censorship.

When Dr. Bowdler set out in the last century to adjust the text of Shakespeare so that no line of the Bard's would ever bring a blush to even the most delicately  nurtured cheek, he furnished Othello with a far, far better reason for strangling Desdemona than anything Shakespeare thought up himself.

What, as justifiable grounds for homicide, can go further than the noble line: "She played the trumpet in my bed"?

122 From a Library Trustee's collection:

A Scottish sleeping-car passenger on the night train from Euston Station, London, to the North sent for the attendant before the train started and explained that it was essential for him to leave the train at Carlisle in the early hours to catch a connection to Dumfries. He explained that he was a heavy sleeper and always reluctant to get up, but stressed the necessity of his leaving the train at Carlisle. The attendant promised to see that the passenger's instructions were obeyed and that the latter could rely on him.

Next morning the passenger awoke to find the train just coming in to Glasgow.

In a fury he rang for the attendant and cursed and swore soundly at him for not putting him off at Carlisle. The attendant listened in silence.

"Man," he said at length, "Ye're a bonny good swearer, but ye're nothing to the man I pit oot at Carlisle."

123 **Well said by an industrial chairman:**

Not many in the House of Commons are worth painting, but some might be better for whitewashing.

The danger of political jokes is that they are sometimes elected.

124 **A Professor of Geography tries a new track:**

This is a New York psychoanalytic joke told to me by a member of the Ford Foundation. It made me laugh, but all academics laugh very loudly at jokes made by Ford Foundation officials.

Mr. F. went to consult Dr. A., the well-known psychoanalyst. "What seems to be your problem, Mr. F.?"

"My problem is, doctor, I can't get on with my wife anymore. Relations between us are a terrible mess. We've talked about a divorce. But before that I thought I should see if you can help."

"Well, Mr. F.," said the great Dr. A., "this is a commoner problem than you'd think. And it proves a real headache to cure. But just lately we've had some interesting reports coming through in the literature. They say that often the real problem is just physical. Truth is, you may be physically run down and you may be worrying about that, so your marriage is going to bits. I can't say that it's the explanation with you, but at least it's worth a try.

"So here's what you should do. I want you to get out of bed tomorrow, get into a track suit, and do a real hard piece of jogging. Exactly ten miles, no more no less. Then the next day exactly the same. Keep it up for one week exactly, ten miles a day. You'll feel pretty terrible because you're badly out of shape. But persevere, and after a week call me to tell me how things work out."

"Doctor, it's worth a trial. I'll do just what you say."

A week later the phone rang in Dr. A.'s office.

"Hello, doctor, this is Mr. F. calling to say I did exactly what you told me. Ten miles a day. It was really tough but I made it and I'm beginning to feel really a lot fitter."

"Great! That's really fantastic. And now the $64,000 question: how are things with you and your wife?"

"How the hell should I know? I'm seventy miles from home."

125 **A Member of Parliament selected this:**

An English Archbishop making his first official visit to the U.S. was duly warned of the dangers of being misquoted by the tough press reporters in America. So he was determined to guard his tongue and when upon arrival at Kennedy Airport he was presented to the throng of reporters in the V.I.P. room, he braced himself for the first question. This came from a tough-speaking reporter, who asked if the Archbishop intended to visit any of the famous New York clubs with their strip tease dancers.

The Archbishop thought carefully for a moment and replied with a little smile: "Are there any such clubs in New York?"

Everyone laughed and applauded, and he was still congratulating himself upon his clever reply the next morning when the newspapers were delivered.

There, staring from the headlines was the bold caption:

Limey Bishop's First Question: "Are there any strip tease clubs in New York?"

The executive was rather gloomy when he got to the office one morning, so his secretary asked him if anything was the matter.

"Nothing really," he said, "but it's my birthday and no one seems to have remembered it."

The secretary sympathized and after a while came back and said:

"Would you like to have a small party with me tonight?"

The executive looked at her and said he would very much like to.

"All right. Come to my flat at about 10 o'clock."

He turned up at the flat on time and was duly admitted by his secretary, looking ravishing, who ushered him in, gave him a drink, and asked him to sit down while she slipped into the next room. After what seemed an age to him she said through the door:

"Nearly ready — just another minute."

Then after a while:

"You can come in now."

He opened the door, and there was a wonderful sight. All his staff were there around a table loaded with food and champagne.

The only trouble was that by this time he only had his socks on.

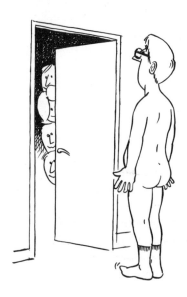

127 A Colonial Governor favors this one:
   A man told his trouble to the psychiatrist.
   "Doctor, I don't know what's wrong with me. I say something, and a minute later I don't remember what I've said."
   "Oh, that's interesting," said the doctor. "How long have you been like this?"
   The man looked at him: "How long have I been like *what*?"

128 A clear answer from a Lord:
   A certain farmer, not renowned for his generosity, gave one of his men during harvest time a glass of beer.
   The man drank it but said nothing; the farmer asked him if it was all right.
   He replied:
   "Just."
   The farmer asked him
   what he meant.
   He replied:
   "If it had been any
   better you wouldn't have
   given it to me; if it had
   been any worse, I couldn't
   have drunk it."

129 A businessman gets a lift out of this:
   Some years ago I visited a small hostelry on the outskirts of Dublin with some friends, and we entered the lounge which was quite simply but comfortably furnished. In one corner of the room was a small hand-operated service lift or elevator with a bell button alongside it bearing the notice "Please ring for service."
   I rang the bell and nothing happened.
   I rang the bell again and still nothing happened.
   I then put my finger on the bell and kept it there, and I could hear it ringing in the basement.
   Suddenly a broad Irish female voice called up the shaft:
   "Are you there, sir?"
   I said: "Yes, I am here."

The voice replied:
"Well, I'll be telling you, the more you will be ringing the more I won't come up."

130 **Limerick from a Colonial officer:**
There was a young lady of
    Wantage
Of whom the Town Clerk
    took advantage
Said the Borough Surveyor
Of course you must pay her
You have altered the line
    of her frontage.

131 **An Earl's toast:**
Toast used for the Ladies:
"Oh, the goodness of their goodness when they're good,
  and the sadness of their sadness when they're sad,
  but the goodness of their goodness
  and the sadness of their sadness
  is as nothing to their badness when they're bad."

132 **A cowboy story from a concert society executive:**
One Sunday in January in one of the midwestern United States, there was a terrible blizzard blowing. The parson struggled through deep snow to the village church where he found a congregation of one — a cowboy in the front pew solemnly chewing gum.

"Well, cowboy," he said, "it's a terrible morning and there are only two of us. Shall we call it a day and get back to our firesides?"

"Well," said the cowboy, "I dunno, I only know about cattle. If I take a load out and only one comes ah still feed him."

Stung by this rebuke, the parson went through the whole morning service, choosing the longer version wherever possible and throwing in a sermon of thirty-five minutes for good measure.

Feeling rather pleased with himself, he again addressed his congregation:

"Well, cowboy, how did I do? Was that all right?"

There was a pause in the rhythmic chewing.

"Well I dunno, I only know about cattle. If I take a load out to feed them and only one comes, ah don't tip the whole load off."

133 Contributed by a Member of the Queen's Bodyguard for Scotland:

The scene is set in Edinburgh about the turn of the century when trolley cars or trams were the normal form of transport.

My mother was getting out of a tram in Princess Street and picked up what she thought was her umbrella, but the lady in the seat beside her said:

"Excuse me but that is mine."

My mother apologized and then picked up her own much inferior one which had fallen on the floor and was hidden by her voluminous skirts of those days.

On her way home from her morning shopping my mother called at a shop to collect her best umbrella, which had been repaired.

On the journey home she found herself sitting in a tram next to the same lady whom she had met earlier. The latter seeing my mother with two umbrellas leaned across and said:

"Ah! I see you have had a successful day."

134 A Crown Agent on red tape:

A civil service assistant received the minutes of a Cabinet meeting, and in accordance with the instruction on them he initialed them and sent them back to the Cabinet office.

Next day they were returned to him with a note:

"It is observed that you have seen and initialed these minutes. You are not authorized to see this class of document. Kindly delete your initials."

He did so and sent the minutes back to the Cabinet office. Next day they were returned to him with another note:

"It is observed that you have made an alteration on this copy of the Cabinet Minutes. Kindly initial it."

135 An M.P. recalls this Churchill incident:

During the last World War when Queen Wilhelmina's country feared German invasion she is reputed to have sent a telegram to Winston Churchill saying:

"Country in grave peril: will flood dikes before allowing invasion by Germans."

Winston Churchill replied:

"Hold your water till jerries arrive."

Signed: "W.C."

136 A Chancellor of the Exchequer exposes a predecessor:

One of my predecessors, as Chancellor of the Exchequer, found it difficult to compose his own after-dinner speeches and therefore delegated the task to his private secretary.

After some years, the worm turned, and when the Chancellor was making his annual speech at the Mansion House, he read it as follows:

"My Lords, Your Grace, My Lord Bishop, My Lords Sheriffs, Ladies and Gentlemen:

"The problem which faces us today is perhaps the most daunting which has ever faced our nation in its island history. Unless we can find a solution in the coming months I see nothing but catastrophe ahead. There are only three possible ways of escape from the dangers now confronting us . . . "

(Then he turned over the page and read out . . . . . .)
"From now on, you're on your own, you bastard!"

137 **A memorable offering from a Brigadier:**
The beautiful countess returned from the ball and rang for her footman. When he came into her bedroom, she said:
"Edward, take off my shoes," and he did.
Then she said: "Edward, take off my coat," and he did.
Next she asked him to take off her dress and then said:
"And now, Edward, take off all my remaining clothes."
When he had done this, the countess said:
"And now, Edward, if you are to remain in my service, you are never to wear my clothes again."

138 **From a solicitor's private stock:**
Coroner to Witness: "The collision occurred at the junction of High Street and Church Road; how far away were you?"
Witness: "54 yards, 2 feet, 6 inches."
Coroner: "You are very precise. Did you measure it?"
Witness: "Yes."
Coroner: "Why?"
Witness: "I knew some idiot would ask me."

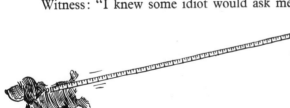

139 **A foreign Ambassador's favorite:**
A tourist, driving a car, arrived in England, and, seeing the yellow line by the side of the road, asked a pedestrian (who happened to be Irish) what it meant.
"Ah, well," he replied, "that means no parking at all."

"Thank you," said the tourist, "but what do two yellow lines mean, then?"

The pedestrian was nonplussed for a moment, but only for a moment.

"Well you see," he said, "that means no parking at all, at all."

Another from the same Ambassador:

A man was out for a walk in one of our larger cities and he met a penguin, which seemed to take a liking to him, as it followed him. Not knowing what to do with it, he took it to the nearest police station and sought advice.

"Take it to the Zoo," they said.

Next day one of the policemen met the man in the street, still accompanied by the penguin.

"What are you doing, still going around with that creature?" he said. "I thought you were going to take it to the Zoo."

"Oh yes," replied the man, "he enjoyed the Zoo, but that was yesterday. Today we are going to the movies."

140 **An Air Chief Marshal donates this:**

Mark Twain was once invited, as the guest of honor, to a dinner at which all the great leaders of the Civil War were present. When it came to the speeches the military leaders made their rather lengthy and somewhat heavy remarks. In due course Mark Twain was called on to speak and he rose — a shade unsteadily — to his feet.

"Gentlemen," he said, "Caesar is dead; Hannibal is no longer with us; Napoleon has long since passed away; and Wellington is under the sod.

"And — to tell you the truth — I am not feeling too good myself."

And with that he sat down.

141 **A foreign Consul likes this best:**
Mother reading letter from greatly adored young son serving with the British Navy as a member of a submarine crew in 1940.

"Dear Mother,

"I am happy to say that I am fit and well and full of life, but unfortunately as you know, I am unable to tell you where I am but you will be interested to know that I shot a polar bear yesterday."

Several weeks later, same mother reading another letter from same son.

"Dear Mother,

"I am happy to say that I am fit and well and thoroughly enjoying myself, but unfortunately as you know, I am unable to tell you where I am but you may be interested to know that last evening I danced with a hula-hula girl."

Same mother reading another letter from same son after a lapse of only two weeks.

"Dear Mother,

"This time I am able to divulge to you that I am in hospital and the doctor tells me that it would have been better had I danced with the polar bear and shot the hula-hula girl."

142 **An air transport official gets off this howler:**
Wife, listening to her husband on the telephone, hears him say indignantly:

"Don't ask me; ask the Coast Guard; ask the Meteorological Office." When he put the phone down she asks:

"Who was that, dear?"

"Some silly ass wanting to know if the coast was clear."

143 **Two revealing notes from a Medical Professor:**
The notice posted in the Town Hall read:
"During the present fuel crisis officials are advised to take advantage of their typists between the hours of 12 and 2."

The newspaper correspondent cabled his editor:
"Almost impossible to exaggerate the gravity of the situation here, but I shall do my best."

144 **An Admiral of the Fleet enjoys this tale:**
A newly commissioned sub-lieutenant was having a drink in the bar one evening when one of his friends came in and complimented him on the cut and style and fit of his uniform. The sub-lieutenant, with a rather self-satisfied smirk, pointed out that he had only just got it from a well-known firm of naval tailors and that it had cost him £150, which accounted for the high quality.

Just as he was about to leave, the other chap said to him:
"I don't know whether you have noticed it or not, but there is one slight flaw — your left trouser leg is longer than your right."

The Sub was furious and stormed into the tailors next morning to be persuaded that to alter the uniform would ruin the style and cut, and that as it was only about an inch too long why not put his left foot on the bar rail when he was next having a drink and hoist up the trouser leg.

The next evening another officer came up to compliment him on one of the smartest uniforms he had seen. The Sub recounted how much it had cost and how pleased he was with it, when the other chap pointed out that the left sleeve was longer than the right.

A quick comparison showed that it was, so next morning he again went back to the tailors to complain. Again he was told that to mess about with minor alterations would ruin the cut and the style, and spoil the suit, and as it had again happened at the bar, why not hold his drink in his left hand, put his elbow on the bar and draw his sleeve down below his cuff.

That evening he was again in the bar with his foot perched on the bar rail, trouser hoisted up, a glass held carefully in his left hand and his sleeve pulled down, when the Commander came in and complimented him on his uniform and said how well turned out he was. The Sub again boasted about the £150, when the Commander said he hardly liked to mention it but there was a small place on the collar of the jacket, which was standing up about an inch above his shirt collar.

The Sub returned to the tailors once more in a terrible rage but was told that this was not uncommon in a new uniform and that, provided he could keep his head slightly lowered for the next few weeks, the collar of the jacket would settle down.

That evening, when having his drink, with his left foot lodged on the bar rail and trouser hoisted, his left hand at an awkward angle over the bar and his head bent forward, he was approached by a midshipman. The midshipman, having complimented him on the cut and style of his uniform, said how much he wished he had gone to the same tailor for his own, but after they had been talking for a little while he said:

"I hope it won't embarrass you being asked this, but how did a chap like you with one short leg, a deformed left arm and a hump on your back get into the Navy, when I had terrible problems just because one of my feet is a bit flat?"

145 **From a banker's collection:**

A young curate was very nervous about giving his first sermon and so the vicar suggested that he should try a little whisky beforehand, but warned the curate not to overdo it. However, the curate was so anxious to be in good form that he took plenty.

Feeling right on top of his form he asked the vicar afterwards how the sermon had gone.

"Well," said the vicar, "you did simply splendidly. There were, however, one or two little points that weren't quite right. First there were twelve Apostles, not ten, and there were ten Commandments, not twelve. Finally, David did not slay Goliath with a ruddy great axe!"

146 A merchant banker charms a listener:

On the occasion when I made my previous speech, a foreign young lady came up to me and said:

"I enjoyed your speech sumptuously."

"Thank you very much."

She went on:

"You ought to have your speeches published."

In as self-deprecating a manner as possible, I said:

"Well, perhaps I will have them published posthumously."

"Oh yes, you should," she answered, "and the sooner the better."

147 Teacher tells all:

The speaker tells how he returns to his school for a class re-union and embellishes this with some nostalgic memories. Because he was principal when the war broke out, he finds himself sitting next to the current principal at dinner. After an excellent dinner at which the wine flows freely, the latter, somewhat advanced in liquor, leans over confidently to the speaker and inquires:

"Let me see, Smith, was it you or your brother who was killed in the last war?"

148 **A former Prime Minister's favorite:**

A man asks his friend:
"How's your wife?"
To receive the answer:
"Compared to what?"

149 **Told by a Chief Admiral:**

The dinner was attended mainly by public relations and advertising people.

In order to stress the importance of their professions I quoted a short rhyme as follows:

The Codfish lays ten thousand eggs
The humble hen lays one,
But the Codfish does not cackle
To tell you what she's done.
And so we scorn the Codfish
While the humble hen we prize,
Which indicates to you and me
It pays to advertise.

150 **An actor gives away a professional secret:**

Two actors playing scene in long-running (too long-running) play. Actors have long since forgotten what play is about. One is thinking:

"Why didn't I make that grand slam in hearts between the shows this afternoon?"

The other:

"Where shall I take my girl friend to supper after the show?"

They dry up.

Prompter blows dust off script and whispers a prompt.
No response.
Prompter gives line a bit louder.
No response.
Third time prompter shouts the prompt.
One of the two actors gets wearily to his feet, crosses to the prompt corner and says to the prompter:
"Yes, darling, we heard you the first time but which of us says it?"

151 **A book publisher's personal favorite:**
A small boy and girl were standing in front of a painting of Adam and Eve in the Garden of Eden.
"Which is Adam and which is Eve?" the girl asked the boy.
"Well, I don't rightly know," the boy replied, "but I think I could tell, if they had their clothes on."

152 **An Army General confesses his love of animals:**
At a private dinner party, during the main course, the dog of the house kept jumping up the male guest sitting on our hostess's left. The dog would put his paws on the man's leg and try and lick him, meanwhile wagging his tail.
With a smug smile the man said to the assembled company:
"You know, it's a funny thing but dogs always love me."
To which our hostess replied:
"I wouldn't be too sure about that. We are rather short of crockery and you are eating off his plate."

153 **Logic from an actor:**
3 a.m. Paddy is awakened by the phone ringing. He gets out of bed and goes downstairs — picks up the phone saying:
"Hello."
"Hello. Is that Belfast double two, double two?"
"No," says Paddy. "This is Belfast two two, two two."
"Ho. I am sorry that you've been troubled."
"It's all right," Paddy replied. "I had to come down as the phone was ringing."

The most precarious profession I have come across involved a man who made his living by hitting crocodiles on the head with a stick with a lump of lead stuck on the end, to knock them out. He lived by a lake in Africa and used to wade out up to waist height at night with a miner's lamp on his head, looking around until the light caught the reflection of a pair of eyes; he would then fasten the light on to the eyes to dazzle them and slowly approach to within three or four feet, at which point the crocodile would make a lunge at him. Stepping smartly to one side, he would hit it as hard as he could just behind one of the eyes with his stick, to knock it out, tie a rope around one leg and tow it off to the shore in order to shoot it with a revolver very carefully, so as not to damage the valuable part of the skin.

There were two hazards to contend with.

The first was when the crocodile woke up on the way to the shore, in which case he was hanging on to a rope with a crocodile with a sore head at the other end; the only thing to do then was to let go of the rope and hope.

The second hazard was that there was no way of telling the difference at night between the eyes of a crocodile and the eyes of a hippopotamus, and it's no use hitting a hippo over the head with anything. They also have a habit of biting people in half. The only clue he got that he was approaching a hippo was when the eyes disappeared under water when he was about four yards away. Hippos don't swim, they bounce along the bottom, which was why

he did not like going deeper than waist high since he liked to feel that he could run faster through a lake than a bouncing hippo, and he did not like the idea of being bitten in half. Unfortunately, one day, or rather night, he was.

The moral may be that if you must live dangerously, do so for something more worthwhile than ladies' handbags.

155 A Welsh Parliamentarian and life in London:

We must always be careful to question the belief, which is current in some quarters, that Governments and great Departments of State know what is best for people.

Some years ago, an Anglesey man from the famous village of Llanerchymedd visited London for the first time. On his first day, he was caught in the rush hour in the Piccadilly Underground station. The confusion was a new experience and he found himself pushed here and there and he lost his hat.

Somehow, he found his way to the street and to a big hat shop. In response to his inquiry, a shop assistant brought four or five new hats for his inspection. After trying them on, he chose one and asked how much it was. On being told that it was five pounds, he said:

"Good Heavens! I could get one exactly like that in Llanerchymedd for thirty shillings."

"That may well be so," replied the assistant, "but you see, we have very large windows here full of hats and sometimes they get faded. We then send them to places like Llanerchymedd, where they are sold cheap."

The Welshman completed the purchase reluctantly, as he had to have a hat, and as he was leaving, the assistant said:

"It *is* a coincidence, but my wife happens to come from Llanerchymedd. She was Ellen Jones and she lived in the Mill. You may have known her?"

"Know her!" he replied, "I knew her well. She was a pretty girl. You won't mind me saying that I took her out for a walk many times."

He paused and then said:

"But when things get a little faded in Llanerchymedd, we send them to London."

156 A Field Marshal reveals his opinion of the medical profession and the Army:

A very successful young tycoon lost his business flair and was so worried he went to his doctor for a medical check-up.

His G.P. could find nothing medically wrong with him and suggested that he should see a brain specialist.

This he did, and was told that his brain was prematurely old and worn out but not to worry as with modern brain transplant surgery he could be given a new one.

He asked about the cost, and the reply was that it all depended on what type of brain he wanted — for instance, he could have a legal brain for $5,000, or a good doctor's brain for $10,000 or an Army officer's brain for $25,000.

"That's preposterous! An officer's brain can't cost more than twice as much as a doctor's!"

"Oh, yes," was the reply. "You see, it's as good as new; it has never been used."

157 A judge and his favorite:

Two men would habitually meet in a pub, but suddenly one of them ceased to come. Months later he reappeared and his friend asked him where he'd been.

"Inside," said Bill.

"Gorblimey, what for?"

"Nothing," said Bill. "It was like this. On my way to work I pass the local police station, and one day a copper put his head out of the gate and asked me to come in. 'What for?' I asked, suspicious-like, though I had a good record. 'To help us,' he said, 'on an identification parade. You just stand in a line and a witness picks out the bloke who done it. It don't take long and you get a cup of tea after.'

"So I went in, curious-like, and a lot just like me sort of stood in a line in the yard. Then a door opened, and the most gorgeous, curvy volupshus young blonde I've ever seen came straight towards us. The bloke in charge said something and she walked down the line. When she came to me, she said, all excited, 'That's him.' 'Touch him on the shoulder,' said the bloke in charge. She did and I felt hot and oozy-like inside."

"Well," said his friend, as Bill seemed wrapped up in his memory, "What happened then?"

"Well," said Bill, "the rest just oozed away and I was taken into the station and a sergeant told me I was under arrest and he was going to charge me. I was still looking at the blue-eyed bundle of she'd-got-it, but the sergeant made me listen to his list."

"Well?" said the friend as Bill again fell silent.

"I l-listened," said Bill, nearly upsetting his beer with emotion at the memory, "and when I heard w-what I had d-done to that g-girl I was so p-proud that I p-pleaded g-guilty."

158 Electronic industrialist gives away current secrets:

In the days when electricity supplies were being converted from direct to alternating current a friend of mine returned from his vacation to find a trench dug along the full length of the road outside his house.

Being of an inquiring disposition he went, after dinner, to see a friend of his who was teaching the classics in school and asked him what was happening.

"I am not quite sure," his friend replied, "but I understand that it is something to do with the electricity — I believe that they are changing us from B.C. to A.D."

159 A statesman takes to the docks:

A rather pompous British politician decided to go on an early-morning tour of the docks in his constituency. It was a bitterly cold morning and, after walking around the wharves for half an hour, the Member of Parliament was "taken short." He went up to a docker standing by the quayside.

"Excuse me, my man," he said, "can you tell me where the urinal is?"

The docker looked him up and down and then replied:
" 'Aven't gotta clue, mate — how many funnels has it got?"

160 **A solicitor reveals a s-l-o-w story:**

A Cambridge professor used to speak so slowly that under-graduates who attended his lectures became bored and impatient and his audiences diminished. At last one of his pupils summoned up courage to tell him candidly, why the lectures were so poorly attended.

"I know . . . I speak . . . so slowly," said the professor, "but my sister . . . speaks . . . much more slowly . . . than I do. She went out one day . . . and she was accosted . . . by a man . . . . She said to him . . . 'I am not that sort of girl . . . at all.' . . . But she spoke too slowly . . . and before . . . she had finished speaking . . . she *was*!"

161 **A tale from a railroad official:**

The speaker was talking about the tension of golf. An important foursome match was tied as it went to the last green. One man was left with a 10-foot putt to halve the match. He studied the line from the back of the hole, he studied it from the front. He lined up to putt. There was a long pause. You could see he was in an agony of concentration and tension. Just as he was taking his stroke a small dog ran between the ball and the hole. The putt went in.

His partner ran over delightedly saying:

"Partner, I don't know how you did it, with that dog running across and all."

"Good heavens," the man replied. "You don't mean to say that was a *real* dog!"

162 **An actor lets fly with a Spoonerism:**

There are innumerable stories (many apocryphal) attributed to Dr. Spooner. The following story, I was assured by the friend who passed it on to me many years ago, is authentic.

Spooner was walking down the High Street one day when he met a young student of his acquaintance, to whom he said:

"Ah, dear man, delighted to see you. Do come to breakfast on Wednesday — I've got Thompson coming."

The young man looked mystified and a little embarrassed. He said:

"It's very kind of you, sir . . . but I *am* Thompson."

To which Spooner replied:

"Oh dear, how very stupid of me — of *course* . . . but do come all the same — I think you'll like him."

From the same actor:

An elephant, crashing through the jungle, noticed a movement near one of his fore-hooves. He stopped and peered down. A tiny creature peeped up at him. The elephant said:

"What are *you*?"

A tiny voice replied:

"I'm a mouse."

Elephant: "You're very *small*."

Mouse: "I know — but I haven't been very well."

163 A headmaster's analysis story:

A headmaster, much concerned about the deteriorating condition of the water in his school swimming bath, sent a sample for analysis to the appropriate authority. The report that came back was:

"This horse is past work and should be destroyed."

164 An organist supplied this pastoral piece:

Two cows are looking over the hedge at the passing traffic and they see among it a large tanker proclaiming in large letters on its side:

"Try our tuberculin-tested milk — pasteurized — sterilized — homogenized."

Buttercup turns ruefully to her neighbor and says:

"I say, Claribel, it makes you feel kind of inadequate, doesn't it."

165 **A union official dips his pen in ink:**

Two Russian workers, Ivan and Boris, were discussing the possibility of going to work at a construction site in Siberia. They had been told that conditions at the site were excellent and that wages were good. However, rather than both of them taking the risk of finding matters less than good, it was agreed that one would go and write to the other.

Ivan lost the toss of the coin and agreed to go. They then discussed the difficulty of the letter which would be sent describing conditions. Ivan said he was not anxious to send a letter saying that conditions were bad and it was agreed that if the letter were written in blue ink it would be true. On the other hand, if it were in red ink it needed to be taken with a large pinch of salt.

Some weeks passed and the letter arrived. Boris observed it was in blue ink and read it with interest.

"Dear Boris.

"The conditions here are very good, safety, health and welfare provided for. The living accommodations are excellent. The supermarket has everything. Fresh bread daily, sausages, pork and every kind of meat. Clothing can be bought cheaply. In fact I can buy many more things here than in Moscow. There seems to be only one shortage. Unfortunately I cannot buy red ink!!"

166 **A composer sets his sights high:**

Candidate on coming out of music examination room:

"I think the examiner must be a very religious man, he keeps putting his head in his hands and saying, 'Oh, my God!' "

167 **Another musician and his high note:**

A matron telling another of the tribulations experienced at her holiday hotel:

". . . . And, my dear, the food there is poison — and such small portions!"

The chairman of the company called the managing director into the board room; he was then followed by the next director in seniority; then by another, and all the way down the line until about half an hour later, the most junior and newly appointed director was duly summoned. He found his colleagues sitting around the board room table.

"Sit down, Charles," said the chairman. "Now then, have you been having an affair with my secretary?"

"Certainly not."

"Are you quite sure?"

"Of course I am. I never laid a finger on her."

"Are you prepared to swear to that?"

"Yes."

"Very well, Charles," said the chairman ominously. "Then *you* fire her!"

169 A logical tale from a leader in the tobacco field:

Among the patients of a certain doctor were a family of mother, father and four children. As he got to know them he was struck by the affection which seemed to unite them all and the happy serenity in which they lived. He was therefore surprised to discover by chance that the parents were not married. Eventually his curiosity got the better of him and he said to the mother:

"I suppose you must have some ideological objection to the state of matrimony, because here you are with a happy, growing family and you are obviously fond of their father and yet you are not married to him."

To which she replied:

"Oh, it's not like that at all. You see, when I was about sixteen I had a spell of heart trouble, which eventually got better and the doctor said I would be all right *provided* I took things gently. I asked him what that meant and, after humming and hawing a bit, he said, 'Well, for example, I think you would be unwise to get married'.

"So me and my Fred decided that it would be safer for me if we skipped the wedding ceremony."

170 A technical expert reports progress:

At a Harvard seminar on the future of profit and industrial relations an American banking president, after listening to me on European movements towards industrial democracy and equity as opposed to the negations and drift in the United States, said: "Jenkins, it isn't *all* bad here. The buffalo are breeding — and the railroads are becoming extinct."

171 A self-definition from a politician:

Marlon Brando is said to have defined an actor as: "A guy who, if you ain't talkin' about him, he ain't listenin'."

To that I would add my own definition of a politician in the same style:

"A politician is a guy, who, if he ain't talking, he ain't listening!"

172 A forestry specialist knows this:

Winston Churchill once said he was flattered when crowds came to hear him speak, except that: "On reflection, the crowds would be even greater if they came to see me hanged."

173 An artist describes a charming encounter:

A young man having gone to some festivity was introduced to a lady and had the temerity to ask for a dance.

After a rather disastrous start he felt it incumbent upon him to make some kind of explanation, and apology — he said: "I'm afraid you'll think me awfully clumsy but I'm a little stiff from badminton."

To which she replied: "I don't care where you come from, but I do wish you'd keep off my feet."

174 An auditor waxes geographical:

The British Colonial Secretary, being asked by a lady admirer: "Mr. Secretary, where are the Virgin Islands?"

Replied after some thought: "Madam, as far away from the Isle of Man as we could put them."

175 An industrialist likes this one:

David and Blodwen had been married for many years but had no children. David went off to work in a local factory while Blodwen stayed at home. One morning she did not feel at all well so went to the doctor. After a thorough examination he said to her:

"Well, Mrs. Davies, I am very pleased to tell you you are pregnant."

Blodwen was delighted — rushed home — picked up the telephone — rang the factory — eventually got through to David's supervisor and said:

"I must speak to David at once — most important — very urgent."

After some delay, the supervisor went up to David and said:

"David, you're wanted on the telephone."

David picked up the telephone and said "Ullo."

Blodwen shouted excitedly down the phone:

"David, I'm pregnant."

Dead silence from David till Blodwen could stand it no longer and shouted:

"David, I tell you I'm pregnant, can't you say something?"
And David said: "Who's speaking?"

176 A gas company executive contributed this:

The Dean of Balliol, A. L. Smith, had several lovely marriageable daughters but often deplored his lack of money.

"But," said a friend, "Your riches are your lovely daughters."
The dean replied:
"But you know one has to husband one's resources."

82

177 Logic from a banker:

Mr. Clark had a telephone message from his bank manager telling him that his bank account was overdrawn by $400 and Mr. Clark said to the bank manager:

"What about it?"

"Don't you realize," said the bank manager, "how serious it is to be overdrawn at our bank?"

"Oh," said Mr. Clark, "What was the state of my account this time last week?"

"I will go and look," said the bank manager.

When he came back he said:

"You were $600 to the good."

"Well," said Mr. Clark, "did I ring you up about it?"

178 A Scottish official gives us this delightful encounter:

In a Highland village there was an Armistice Day gathering attended by all the local clergy and other big-wigs, and the laird of the manor and his wife offered refreshments afterwards. At the end of the service the bishop made a smart getaway to the Big House and was already sitting in the inglenook with a goblet in his hand when the Free Kirk minister arrived.

"Ah, Mr. MacTavish," cried the hostess, "will you take a dram this cold morning?"

The minister raised his hands in horror. "My dear lady," he said, "I never touch spirits. I would as soon commit adultery as drink a glass of whisky."

The bishop looked up from his corner. "Your ladyship," he said, "didn't tell me that there was a choice."

179 From the same Scottish official:

There was a traveling circus that owned a gorilla. He was their pride and joy, but he pined for his African forests, and when they set out on a tour of the Highlands, he lay down and died. The circus men did not think it would do to arrive in Inverness with a dead gorilla, so in the Pass of Drumochter, in the middle of the night, they left the poor creature in the ditch.

Early next morning along came two Highland bumpkins, and stopped short at this foreign apparition.

"Whit like is this, Angus?" said one.

The other took off his tam (out of reverence) and scratched his head.

"I'm not rightly knowing, Donald," he said, "yon's no red enough for a MacGregor."

"Aye, Angus, but a Campbell would be blacker."

"Ye're no thinking it's a MacAulay, are ye, it's too big for that."

So they puzzled each other, until at last Angus said:

"I'll tell you whit way it is, Donald, we'll juist nip off to the hotel and see if ony of they English visitors is missing."

180 A physician shares a puzzle:

Two African doctors were walking along a river in Africa when they suddenly saw a drowning man. They rushed to help him, brought him to the bank, resuscitated him with mouth-to-mouth breathing and then found a wagon to take him the many miles to the nearest hospital for treatment.

They then went back and started their walk again, only to find another drowning man. Having gone through exactly the same procedure, they got back to the river bank only to find yet one more drowning man. After resuscitating him and then another, they found they were doing this all day.

At this point one of the doctors said to the other:

"This is a place we must build a hospital because this is the place where people drown."

The other one then started to walk upstream, when he heard a shout from his colleague:

"Hey, come quickly, there is another drowning man."

Undeterred, he continued his walk upstream, saying:

"I'm going to find out who is pushing them in!"

181 A diplomat unlocks a Spanish secret:

A British businessman visiting an office in Madrid at 3 p.m. one weekday was disconcerted to find no one on duty. He roused the caretaker in the basement and asked:

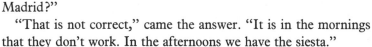

"Do they not work in the afternoons in Madrid?"

"That is not correct," came the answer. "It is in the mornings that they don't work. In the afternoons we have the siesta."

182 A Member of Parliament discourses on true grit:

At a recent N.A.T.O. meeting three admirals were conferring and discussing the nature of courage. They could not agree.

"I vill show you vat is ze nature of courage," expostulated the German admiral, summoning one of his lieutenants to him.

"You see zat 100-meter flagpole over zere? I vish you to climb to ze top, salute, and jump off!"

The German officer immediately obeyed, ran to the flagpole, climbed swiftly up, saluted smartly and jumped down.

"Well, that is very impressive," said the American admiral, "but let me now show you what we have come to regard as courage in the history of the United States Navy." Summoning an American lieutenant, he said:

"You see that 200-meter flagpole! I want you to climb to the top of that flagpole, salute twice and jump off."

At the double the American officer carried out the command, climbed to the top, saluted and jumped off.

"Well, gentlemen, that was a jolly impressive show," said the British admiral, "but I shall now show you the nature of courage as we understand it in the Royal Navy."

Calling to an enlisted sailor he told him:

85

"You see that 300-meter flagpole over there? I want you to climb to the top, salute three times, and jump off."

"What, me, sir?" responded the sailor in a tone of incredulity, "You must be bloody daft, sir!"

"There, gentlemen," said the British admiral, "we have the true nature of courage."

183 A journalist reveals how to take it with you:

A rich industrialist from New York City expressed the wish to be buried in Miami in his gold-plated Cadillac.

Came the day, he was dressed in his white tuxedo suit and laid in the car. An enormous hole was dug in the ground and the Cadillac (with contents) hoisted thirty feet up, ready for the big drop.

"Gee," said one of the onlookers, "that's livin'!"

184 Quick thinking intrigued a tourist official who likes this story:

A doctor driving along a freeway in his high-powered car and well in excess of the speed limit happened to see through his car mirror the fast approach of a police patrol car.

Rightly assuming that its occupants were intent on pulling him in for speeding, he quickly picked up his stethoscope, which was conveniently at hand, and, as they drove alongside, he dangled it for the police officers to see. Taking due note, they saluted politely and drew away.

The same doctor returned an hour or two later along the same route and at the same high speed. But this time he was unaware that the same police officers were once more in hot pursuit.

Just as he realized what was happening the patrol car drove past and as it did so one of the officers leant out and in his turn dangled before the doctor's eyes — a pair of handcuffs!

185 **A pianist plays this sad tune:**
The marriage broker introduces his client to the young lady selected as a prospective bride. The client finds her shockingly unattractive, and during dinner lists her shortcomings to his friend in an angry whisper. He says:

"How could you do this to me! She is monstrous, she squints, she has a beard, she is almost deformed, she . . . ."

The broker interrupts him:

"You needn't whisper. She's deaf, too."

186 **From a distinguished jurist:**
Drunken voice, over the telephone:
"Is that Alcoholics Anonymous?"
"Yes. Do you wish to join?"
"No. I want to resign."

187 **Comparisons from a banker:**
A somewhat loquacious gentleman who had been invited to reply for the guests at a large public dinner gradually became pretty well inebriated during the course of the meal, and by the time he had to get to his feet, he did so with considerable difficulty, and his speech was extremely slurred and difficult to understand. In addition to that, it went on for a very long time before he finally collapsed back into his chair.

At that stage, he turned to the gentleman sitting next to him and asked him what he thought of his speech, to which the reply came:

"Rolls-Royce."

The speaker looked much perplexed and said:

"Why do you call it Rolls-Royce?"

His neighbor said:

"Well, in the first place it was so silent I could hardly hear it, secondly it was extremely well oiled, and thirdly I thought it was going to last forever."

188 **A judge who is a weekend sailor knocks this one off:**

A keen yachtsman took his friend, whose main recreational hobby was game shooting, out for a sail in his boat. The wind changed direction suddenly and the boat was about to jibe.

The yachtsman yelled: "Duck!"

His friend stood up and said "Where?" — and was knocked overboard by the boom.

The same judge has this one for the road:

A man went into a pub.

"Good evening, sir," said the bartender, "what will you have?"

"Thank you, a large whisky," said the man.

After he had drunk it the bartender asked for payment.

"Oh, no," said the man, "I distinctly remember — you invited me to have a drink; I thought it was very kind of you."

The bartender, who was also the owner, turned to the only other customer present, who was a solicitor, and asked for support.

The solicitor placed his fingertips together and after thinking awhile said:

"He's right you know, there was an offer and acceptance — and that's a contract."

The bartender, furious, ordered the man out of his pub, never to return. A little while later the man returned.

"I thought I told you never to come back again!" said the bartender.

"Never been here in my life before," said the man.

The bartender, very puzzled but apologetic said:

"Well, all I can say is that you must have a double!"

"Thanks very much," said the man, "and I'm sure our solicitor friend here will have one too."

189 A professor finds a generous Scot:
   The principal of a Scottish university early in this century visited a primary school arrayed in full academic dress.
   "Who am I?" he asked the class:
   "A penny for the boy who knows who I am."
   Silence: and then a solitary suggestion:
   "Ye're God."
   "No; I'm no' God; but here's tuppence."

190 Reportage Russian style via an industrialist:
   During an afternoon of relaxation at an international conference, to settle a bet, a race took place between the British and the Russian Ambassadors.
   "The Times" reported it thus:
   "A race took place between the British and the Russian Ambassadors. The British Ambassador won."
   "Izvestia" reported it thus:
   "A race took place between Ambassadors. The Russian Ambassador came in second. The British Ambassador was last but one."

191 As an Air Marshal tells it:
   A very elderly soccer enthusiast decided at the age of 85 to emigrate to Australia because, he said, the growth of homosexuality appalled him.
   He recalled as a boy how he heard it was punishable by hanging.
   He knew as he grew older that the punishment had been reduced to a flogging. Forty years ago it had been further reduced to imprisonment, thirty years ago to a fine, and now that it was no longer illegal he wished to leave the country before it was made compulsory.

192 Courtesy of a clever diplomat:
   As a practical demonstration of the terms "circulation of money" and "re-distribution of wealth" a business man gave each of his two teenage sons $10 with an injunction to use the money to best advantage and report the result at the end of a fortnight.

On due date the elder son announced that he had doubled his capital, for which he was paternally commended.

The younger son, however, admitted to having nothing left, explaining ruefully that he had lost all $10 to his elder brother at poker.

193 **Verse from a philosophical Secretary of the Admiralty:**
The horse and mule live thirty years
   And nothing know of wines or beers.
The goats and sheep at twenty die
   With never a taste of scotch or rye.
The cow drinks water by the ton
   And at eighteen is mostly done.
The dog at sixteen cashes in
   Without the aid of rum or gin.
The cat in milk and water soaks
   And then in twelve short years it
      croaks
The sober, modest, bone-dry hen
   Lays eggs for nogs, then dies at ten.
The animals are strictly dry
   They sinless live and swiftly die.
While sinful, ginful, rum-soaked men
   Survive for three score years and ten.
And some of us, though mighty few
   Stay pickled till we're ninety-two.

194 **As it happened to a medical adviser:**
The colonel was known to be on the mean side, and I was hardly surprised at the single pre-dinner glass of rather thin sherry offered to me.

Less expected, however, in spite of the colonel's reputation, was his behavior when the dish containing the two deliciously grilled fresh trout arrived. One fish was conspicuously longer than the other, but, without a blush, the colonel served me with the small fish. I could not resist making some comment:

"Colonel," I said, "is this quite the thing to do?"

"What do you mean?" asked the colonel.

"Well," I replied, "if you were my guest, I would give you the large fish and keep the small fish for myself!"

"But, damn it!" said the colonel, "you've *got* the small fish, haven't you?"

195 **A judge's two favorites:**
Belinda Smith, aged five, was, much to her mother's concern, always telling lies. One day she came home and gave a graphic account of her meeting with a lion in the road.

After much trouble and tears she admitted that it was only a dog. Her mother told her that she must ask God's forgiveness.

After her prayers that night, asked whether she had done so, she said:

"Yes, and do you know what God said? He said, 'Don't mention it, Miss Smith, I have often made the same mistake myself.' "

Late at night a police officer was checking stationary cars, and their occupants, in a quiet street. In one he saw a young man reading a book in the front seat and a girl knitting in the back seat.
Policeman: "What are you doing here?"
Young man: "Can't you see, reading a book."
Policeman: "How old are you?"
Young man: "Twenty."
Policeman: "What is she doing in the back?"
Young man: "Can't you see, knitting."
Policeman: How old is she?"
Young man: (looking at watch)
"In eleven minutes time she will be eighteen."

A company chairman who was given a ticket for a performance of Schubert's Unfinished Symphony couldn't go, and so he passed on the invitation to the company's work study consultant. The next morning the chairman asked him how he enjoyed it, and instead of a few plausible observations was handed a memorandum which read:

(a) For considerable periods the four oboe players had nothing to do. The number should be reduced, and their work spread over the whole orchestra, thus eliminating peaks of inactivity.

(b) All twelve violins were playing identical notes. This seems unnecessary duplication, and the staff of this section should be drastically cut. If a large volume of sound is really required this could be obtained through an electronic amplifier.

(c) Much effort was absorbed in the playing of demi-semi-quavers. This seems an excessive refinement, and it is recommended that all notes should be rounded up to the nearest semiquaver. If this were done it should be possible to use trainees and low-grade operators.

(d) No useful purpose is served by repeating with horns the passage that has already been handled by the strings. If all such redundant passages were eliminated, the concert could be reduced from two hours to twenty minutes.

If Schubert had attended to these matters, he would probably have been able to finish his symphony after all!

Milton said: "Hard are the ways of truth."

A young naval sub-lieutenant awaiting his court martial, may well have echoed that poet's sentiments.

His ship had put into a foreign port and he had been given half a day's shore leave. There was a coal mine near the port and he thought it would be interesting to go down it. So he obtained permission from the manager of the mine, changed into the appropriate clothes and spent most of his leave down in the mine.

Eventually he came up, bathed and changed and, looking spick and span, started off towards his ship.

He had not gone far when he was accosted by one of his senior officers, who asked him if he would take his golf clubs and put them in the officer's cabin. He of course agreed, took the clubs and went on his way to his ship.

It so happened that when he arrived he found that the Admiral in charge of the Fleet was paying his ship a visit and was standing by the gangway.

This Admiral was a very cantankerous old man and usually took no notice whatever of officers of lowly rank, except to acknowledge their salutes.

The young man was a little dismayed at seeing the Admiral but there was nothing about it and so, first taking a quick look to see that his uniform was in order and adjusting the bag of golf clubs so as to make his general appearance as satisfactory as possible, he strode up the gangway and saluted the Admiral smartly.

For once the old man was in a benevolent mood and instead of grunting in reply to the young man's "Good evening, sir" he said:

"Hullo, my boy. Been playing golf?"

"No, sir," replied the young man, "I've been down in a coal mine," and was immediately put under arrest for insubordination.

198 **High note from a Commanding General:**

An English opera singer was once invited to sing at La Scala in Milan.

After completing his first aria, a particularly well-known one, he was greeted with shouts of:

"Encore!"

So he sang it again and this time the shouts were even louder.

After the third time when the same thing happened and he had taken his bow, he stepped to the front of the stage, held up his hand for silence, and said:

"Ladies and Gentlemen, thank you for your wonderful reception. I am deeply touched that you should have received me in this way on my first visit to Milan. But now, if you will allow me to do so, we must continue with the opera."

At this, a man stood up at the back of the audience and shouted: "No! No! You do notta understand. We donta want you to stop! We wanta you to go on until you getta it right!"

199 **An industrial engineer works out a solution:**

Jack was talking to George one day and saying how he and his wife were at daggers drawn.

"I really can't stand it," he said, "I would cut her throat, but then of course I would have to swing for that."

"Not at all," said George, "there are easier ways. You buy her a motor-bike and she'll do herself in with that."

So Jack bought his wife a fast motor-bike.

George meanwhile was away on business for a while. On his return he inquired at once about Jack's problem, only to be told that the wife was getting on marvelously with the motor-bike and having a wonderful time with it. So George suggested Jack should buy her a Jaguar and see if that would do the trick.

Again George was away for a while and returned, anxious to know how his friend's wife was getting on.

This time Jack was able to say:

"It's marvelous — the jaguar bit her head off!"

200 **An author's prerogative:**

A woman went to see her lawyer, taking with her a baby in arms and four other children under the age of five.

"And what can I do for you?" he said.

"I want a divorce," she replied.

"And on what grounds?"

"Desertion, sir."

"Desertion, madam?"

He looked from her to each of the five children in turn.

"Oh, don't take any notice of them," she confided. "He really *has* deserted me. Only every now and then he comes home to apologize."

201 From a learned judge:

It was a small Highland church. The minister, one of the old school, was in full flight and was not sparing in his castigation of his flock . . .

"And there shall be much weeping and gnashing of teeth. . . ."

An old rebel, one Hamish Macgregor, whose last tooth had deserted him many years ago, grinned up at the preacher.

The challenge was accepted, and, transfixing the recalcitrant with an eagle eye, the old divine thundered:

"Do not fool yoursel', Hamish Macgregor. Teeth will be provided."

202 A physician's Rx:

A lawyer was advised by his doctor to give up all forms of alcohol as part of the treatment for his dyspepsia. Five years later, visiting the same doctor but now complaining of insomnia he was told to take a nightly shot of whisky.

The lawyer, a man of good memory, pointed out that the previous advice was to avoid alcohol completely.

The doctor, a man of resource, replied:

"Ah, yes, but medicine has made great strides since those days."

203 Courtesy of a building executive:

Members of the church committee were just finalizing arrangements for the summer fete to be held on the following day.

Checking through the list of V.I.P.'s someone noted that a wealthy lady in the village had not been invited.

The vicar hastily wrote a note and sent a choir boy around with it. The lady saw the boy coming up the driveway on his bicycle and went to the door with the greeting:

"Too late, young man, I've already prayed for rain."

204 A judge confesses his confusion:

Just after my appointment as a judge I was booking into an hotel.

The receptionist asked my name, which I gave as "Lonsdale," and she started to write in the hotel register "Mr. Lonsdale."

"Excuse me," I said, "Judge."

So she crossed out "Mr. Lonsdale" and, saying "I do wish you'd make up your mind what your name is," wrote down "Mr. Judge."

205 From a member of the diplomatic corps, who learned his lesson well:

The Roman Emperor was enjoying a splendid afternoon's sport, watching the Christians being devoured by the lions.

Suddenly he was astonished to see one of the lions bounding up to his victim who, however, bent down and appeared to whisper something in the animal's ear, whereupon the lion turned around and slunk away.

As the Emperor watched, the same thing happened again and again; this particular Christian would say something quietly to the lion, and the latter would promptly retreat from where he came.

At last the Emperor's curiosity could stand it no longer. He sent for the Christian and promised to spare his life if only he would reveal what it was that he whispered to the lions to produce this extraordinary effect.

"Well," replied the Christian, "it's really quite simple, Your Majesty. I just say to them 'Of course, you realize that after you've dined you'll have to make a speech.' "

206 A book publisher's note:

The broad-minded vicar was invited by the broad-minded headmistress to talk to her older girls about Christianity and sex. Not wishing to compromise either his diary or his less tolerant wife he entered the engagement as "Talk to girls about sailing."

96

A day or so after his talk the headmistress encountered the vicar's wife.

"So very good of your husband to talk to my girls the other evening. He was quite splendid and so helpful."

"I can't imagine what he knows about it," replied the vicar's wife, "he's only done it twice and the first time he was sick and on the second occasion his hat blew off."

207 **Thanks to an economist for this one:**

The famous Mr. Justice Avory had just sentenced a hardened old rogue to 20 years' imprisonment — not uncommon in his time. Although a great judge, he looked as if he was asleep on the bench. Small and terrifying, he was known as the "hanging judge," somewhat unfairly.

The old rogue said: "But, my Lord, I shall not live that long."

Mr. Justice Avory replied: "Well do your best, my man."

208 **An industrialist contributed this:**

One judge by the name of Lord Fraser wished to borrow a book one evening and for that purpose he sent his butler to the house of his colleague, Lord Young.

Lord Young, who had a well-known sharp wit, said he had the book and he would be delighted to lend it to Lord Fraser.

Before handing it over, however, he wrote his name on the flyleaf and, pointing to his signature as he handed the book to the butler, said:

"Will you please tell Lord Fraser, that I do not in the slightest doubt his honesty. This is merely an instruction to his executors."

209 From an Air Force Minister:

A Scottish law lord was principal guest at a clan dinner. On rising to make the main speech of the evening he made a number of conventional remarks about "What an honor it was," "How much he enjoyed meeting, etc.," and so on, and went on to praise the excellence of the food and wine. He then continued (roughly):

"Notwithstanding your almost overwhelming hospitality, I will claim that although I may not be as sober as a judge, I am at least not as drunk as a lord."

210 Chuckles from a Professor of Education:

A prominent politician from a newly independent Pacific island territory was on his first luxury voyage on a P. & O. liner to Britain, where he was to present his credentials to Her Majesty, as Ambassador.

Very large, very black, fierce and primitive of appearance, and with a highly developed sense of humor, he entered the dining salon on the first evening and watched the steward approach him with obvious trepidation.

He scanned the ample menu for several minutes and then said in booming tones:

"No, nothing here for me, thank you — bring me the passenger list."

and another from the same professor:

I was once involved in the recruitment of a night watchman for a university in an African country in which alcohol presented very serious problems. Towards the end of one interview of what seemed a highly promising applicant, the registrar popped one of the crucial questions:

"Mr. Mukasa, if you are to be responsible for university security, we need to know a little about your personal habits. Tell me, for example, do you drink?"

There was a long pause while our would-be colleague ruminated. Then he replied, with disarming candor:

98

"No sir, I do not drink. I have tried drinking, but I found that I did not like it. However, if you think it is important, I will try again."

211 **An electrical engineer throws light on this:**

The local midwife was attending the wife of Sandy, a Highland shepherd, at his cottage in a remote glen, relying on the light from a fitful candle.

Two babies were successfully delivered when the candle began to gutter.

"Get me a new candle," shouted the midwife to Sandy.

"Na, Na," replied Sandy, "I'll no' be a party to replacing the licht. It may be attractin' them."

212 **Ale to the judge:**

Irish barmaid: "I'm sorry, sir, the bar will not be open for half an hour — would you like a drink while you're waiting?"

213   Two gems from a Scottish banker, chief clansman:

There was a long-winded speaker who was addressing with difficulty an unruly gathering in the Scottish Highlands. He held up his hands for silence and, when this was grudgingly given, he said:

"I am speaking not only to you but to generations yet unborn."

There was a pause and then a voice from the hall called out:

"If you don't hurry up, they will soon all be here."

A Presbyterian minister was known for his abstinence from alcoholic beverages. One evening, after a particularly good dinner with one of his elders, he was, however, persuaded to take just one small glass of cherry brandy.

After one or two had been consumed and enjoyed, his host promised to send a couple of bottles around to the manse provided the reverend gentleman acknowledged the gift in the parish magazine.

This was duly promised and the next edition of the magazine contained the following announcement:

"Your minister wishes to acknowledge and express his thanks for the most welcome gift of fruit and the spirit in which it was given."

214   An Irish barrister on the merits of fresh air and sun:

In Ulster, the custom of the funeral wake is still observed.

The man had been rather ill, and his wife took him off for a month's vacation at the seaside, where they enjoyed excellent weather.

The day after he got home, he had a fatal coronary.

At his wake his friends queued up to take their leave of the departed, lying in an open coffin. One woman, having gazed fondly down at him for a minute or two, turned to the widow and said gushingly:

"Oh, doesn't he look lovely? You can see that holiday at Portrush did him a world of good."

215 **This rib-tickler from a Major-General in the Marines:**
Five men are in an aircraft. A priest, a professor, a mountaineer, complète with rucksack, a writer, and the pilot.

Suddenly the pilot comes into the cabin, announces engine failure and that the aircraft is about to crash. He regrets there are only four parachutes but is sure they must all realize it is vital for him to report down below the cause of the crash. He grabs a parachute and jumps to safety.

The priest says he has a flock of five thousand souls to look after and he is a very important person to them. He grabs the second parachute and out he jumps.

Then the professor steps forward and says he has to represent his country in the Brain of the World competition next month so for its sake he feels he has to take a parachute. So saying he jumps.

The writer turns to the mountaineer and says:

"Well, old boy, one 'chute left. What do we do now?"

"Don't worry, my friend," he says, "there are still two 'chutes, the bloody Brain took my bloody rucksack."

216 **A writer submits a scientific puzzle and a logical solution:**
Here is the way a question was asked in physics in a degree exam at the University of Copenhagen: "Describe how to determine the height of a skyscraper with a barometer."

One student answered as follows:

"You tie a long piece of string to the neck of the barometer, then lower the barometer from the roof of the skyscraper to the ground. The length of the string, plus the length of the barometer, will equal the height of the skyscraper."

This highly original answer so incensed the examiner that he failed the student for being cheeky. The student appealed to the university authorities on the ground that his answer was indisputably correct, and that he should have been given full marks.

The university appointed an impartial arbiter to decide the case, a visiting professor from the University of Washington. He ruled that although the answer was technically correct, it did not display any noticeable knowledge of physics; and to resolve the matter, he called the student in and gave him six minutes in which to answer the question verbally in a way that showed at least a minimal familiarity with the basic principles of physics.

For five minutes there was complete silence. The student sat there frowning heavily, deep in thought. The professor reminded him that time was running out, to which the student replied that he had several extremely relevant answers to the question, but could not make up his mind which one of them was best.

"You had better hurry up," he was told.

"All right then," said the student. "You take the barometer up to the roof of the skyscraper, drop it over the edge, and measure the time it takes to reach the ground. The height of the building can then be worked out in terms of the formula $H = \frac{1}{2}gt^2$ (height equals one half times the gravity-time squared). But bad luck on the barometer.

"Or if the sun happens to be shining, you could measure the height of the barometer, then set it up on end and measure the length of its shadow. Then you measure the shadow of the sky-scraper, and thereafter it is a simple matter of proportional arithmetic to work out the height of the skyscraper.

"But if you wanted to be highly scientific about it, you could tie a short piece of string to the neck of the barometer and swing it like a pendulum, first at ground level and then on the roof of the skyscraper, and work out the height of the building by the difference in the gravitational restoring force $(T = 2\pi$ square root of l over g).

"Or if the skyscraper had an outside emergency staircase, it would be easier simply to walk up it and mark off the height of the skyscraper with a pencil, in barometer-lengths, and then add them up.

"If you merely wanted to be boring and orthodox about it, of course, you could use the barometer to measure the air pressure on the roof of the skyscraper, compare it with standard air-pressure on the ground, and convert the difference in millibars into feet to give you the height of the skyscraper.

"But since we are constantly being exhorted to exercise independence of mind and apply scientific methods, undoubtedly the best way would be to knock on the janitor's door and say to him, 'If you would like a nice new barometer, I will give you this one if you tell me the height of this skyscraper.' "

217 A diplomat reminisces:

I was sitting with another old man, a friend of mine, gazing with lackluster eyes out of the windows in our club, when a very pretty girl came along, walking fast down the street. Immediately after, walking rather faster, came a personable young man in hot pursuit.

"Did you see that?" I said. "That young man, chasing that pretty girl? Do you remember how you and I used to chase pretty girls?"

Listlessly he looked at me and said:

"Yes, I remember *how* we used to chase them, but I can't remember *why*."

218 From a Colonel and city official:

My wife was sitting at the end of a platform at an English-Speaking Union meeting when she fell. A bishop was standing by and caught her in his arms and said:

"This is the first time I have had a fallen woman in my arms."

And she said:

"This is the first time I have been picked up by a bishop."

219 **A law professor likes this brief example:**

A friend of mine, an American judge has, like many such, a court in matrimony. He tells how, one Saturday afternoon, the chores of the week all over, he was taking it easy when a most charming young couple were shown in.

The boy, almost stifled by nervousness, said:

"Judge, we've come to ask you to marry us."

"Yes," replied the judge, "I should be delighted to do so," but went on to explain that he could not do so before Monday, because the bureau which alone could issue a marriage license was closed until then.

The young couple, utterly crestfallen, retreated to a far corner of the studio and held a whispered, but obviously agitated, conversation.

They returned in a moment or two, this time with a most determined young woman drawing along an obviously reluctant young man.

"We quite understand, Judge," she said, smiling sweetly, "we quite understand you can't *really* marry us until Monday, but do you think you could say a few words that would tide us over the weekend . . . . . . ?"

220 **A banker tells this one on bankers:**

An investment banker hired a plumber to repair a faucet. He took ten minutes on the job and charged $50.

"I say," said the investment banker, "I couldn't make $50 for ten minutes work."

"Nor could I," said the plumber, "when I was an investment banker."

221 From the files of a Circuit Judge:

Early in the Great War, Queen Mary visited a certain military hospital. She stopped at the bedside of a rifleman, who had lost a leg at the first Battle of Ypres, and asked where it had happened.

"At Vipers, Ma'am," said the wounded warrior.

"Ypres, my man," said The Queen.

During the conversation which followed, Her Majesty encouraged the soldier to tell the whole of his story, and on each occasion that he mentioned "Vipers" corrected him gently:

"Ypres, my man."

When the visit was over, the nurse in charge of the ward inquired of her patient how he had got on with The Queen.

"Oh, she was very nice," said the rifleman, "but the poor lady had terrible hiccups."

222 The Queen's Surgeon takes time off to tell this:

A married couple bring their daughter, aged about eight, up to London to do some shopping. Among other purchases she bought a pair of red shoes which she insists on wearing.

On the way home, going up in the elevator at Waterloo, a woman immediately in front of them suddenly, and for no apparent reason, slaps the face of the man standing next to her. There is quite a scene. At the top, the ticket collector tries to calm them down but fails, other passengers join in and eventually police appear.

The parents and little girl hurry off to catch their train and, having got into their seats, start discussing this strange affair.

Suddenly the child says: "I didn't like that woman."

"Why not?" asks the mother.

"She stepped on my new shoes," says the child, "so I gave her bottom a good pinch."

223 A Postmaster General defends the male:

Guests in a Cairo hotel, hearing a scream in the corridor, discovered a damsel in a négligée being pursued by a gentleman who was, to put it bluntly, nude.

Later it developed that the impetuous Romeo was an English major, who was promptly court-martialed.

His lawyer won him an acquittal, however, by virtue of the following paragraph in the army manual:

"It is not compulsory for an officer to wear a uniform at all times, as long as he is suitably garbed for the sport in which he is engaged."

224 A Member of Parliament tells this:

An earnest temperance lady was carrying out a survey of drinking habits.

She rang the bell of a house and a bluff colonel answered.

She explained:

"I am doing a survey into people's drinking habits. If you don't object" — she was a very polite investigator — "would you mind giving me some information about yours?"

"Not at all," replied the colonel. "The fact is that I haven't had a drink since 19.45."

"Congratulations, indeed," said the lady, effusively, "that is quite a remarkable achievement."

"I know," responded the colonel, looking at his watch. "It is already 20.00 hours."

225 **A development executive with loss for words:**
Noah Webster was the founder and compiler of "Webster's Dictionary" and was naturally a "stickler" for words — and incidentally, for his secretary.

The two of them were one day locked in fond embrace, when Mrs. Webster happened to burst into his office.

"Oh, Noah, I *am* surprised," exclaimed the good lady.

"No, my dear, you are wrong again," responded Webster. "It is *we* who are surprised. *You*, surely, are astounded."

226 **A Member of Parliament gives this as an example of reliability:**
A Member of Parliament was constantly in trouble with his wife at home and his Chief Whip in the House of Commons. The reason that he was invariably late for his meals and missing his votes in the House was the problem of his car, which kept breaking down.

So he decided to visit a car showroom. He stated that he wanted a car that was absolutely "reliable and dependable" — and explained his problem.

The showroom salesman said:

"We have just the car for you, sir," and showed him a Rolls-Royce.

The M.P. had a look, opened the trunk and saw a spare tire and a kit of tools.

"What are those for?" he said. "You tell me that this car is absolutely reliable and dependable — so why a spare tire and kit of tools?"

"Well, sir," said the salesman, "we always supply a set. Just in case!"

"Just in case?" repeated the M.P. "Where's the reliability and dependency?"

"Well, we always do," said the salesman.

But no matter how he explained, the M.P. was not satisfied. So in sheer exasperation the salesman said:

"Look, sir, when you go into your bathroom in the morning and strip to the waist, you look into the mirror and you see" —

pointing to his chest — "a red spot here and a red spot there. Now you know that you are not going to have a baby and so do I — but they are there 'just in case'!"

227 **A Professor of Engineering delves into the archives:**
Successive headlines appeared in the Paris newspapers when Napoleon landed with his army on the south coast of France.
1. Corsican Fiend Lands at Marseilles.
2. Bonaparte takes Orléans.
3. Marshal Napoleon at the Gates of Paris.

228 **So speaks the Speaker of the House of Commons:**
The mean man went to stay with his friend. After dinner his friend said:
"Would you like some coffee?"
"No — tea," he replied.
Late that evening his friend asked him:
"Would you like a nightcap of whisky?"
"No — brandy," he replied.
Next morning his friend asked him:
"Would you like tea with your breakfast?"
"No — coffee," he replied.
His friend then asked:
"How would you like your eggs, scrambled or fried?"
"One fried, one scrambled," he replied.
After breakfast his friend asked him:
"Did you enjoy your breakfast?"
"No," he replied. "You scrambled the wrong egg."

229 A Nobel Prize Winner in Medicine waxes anatomical:

A well-known public school was recently obliged to raise its fees by several hundred pounds per annum. All parents were notified of this by a secretary who unfortunately wrote "per anum" instead of "per annum."

One indignant parent wrote back and said he thanked the headmaster very much for the notification of the recent increase in fees, but for his part he would prefer to go on paying through the nose as usual.

230 A politician and diplomat becomes pejorative:

Smythe-Ffoulkes and Mainwaring-Dalrymple went to the same prep school, and took an instant and lasting dislike to one another.

The dislike deepened as they went through public school and university together, and then separated ostensibly for the rest of their lives.

S-F went into the Church, and in the fullness of time became a bishop.

M-D went into the Navy, and he, in due course, became an admiral.

One day Bishop Smythe-Ffoulkes was waiting at Bath station: he had been to an investiture and was in full episcopal robes. At the far end of the platform he saw a resplendent figure in admiral's uniform. Could it be, yes it must be, that unspeakable Mainwaring-Dalrymple.

He thought for a moment. Then he went up to the admiral.

"Tell me, stationmaster," he said, "when does the next train go to London?"

The admiral, too, had recognized his former pet aversion.

"It goes in ten minutes, madam," he replied, "but in your condition I don't think you ought to be traveling."

231 Chuckles from a TV broadcaster, who collects these:

A collection of quotations from various holiday brochures:

If this is your first visit to our hotel you are welcome to it.

You will not be likely to forget quickly your experience with us.

Situated in the shadiest part of the town, you cannot fail to notice from the window the odors of the pine trees and our swimming pool.

If you wish for breakfast, lift the telephone, ask for room service, and this will be enough for you to bring your food up.

On gala nights the chef throws his best dishes, and all water used in cooking has been passed by the manager personally.

If your wife needs something to do, she should apply to our suggestive head porter, but all of our staff are courteous, and to ladies too attentive.

We would very much like to have relations with you, and we will be most happy to dispose of all your clients.

232 A diplomatic gesture:

There was once a very hungry raffish Tom Cat. Although he was ugly and torn and scarred, the Pussy Cats adored him for his rough forthright approach. But he kept everyone awake for miles around.

The neighbors decided something had to be done. One night he disappeared. He had been kidnapped and sent away to be "doctored."

The Pussies mourned him for many a long moonlit night.

Then suddenly a new fat silky cat turned up in Tom's old haunts. Yes, it was Tom himself! A thousand amorous mewings were heard. But Tom was unmoved.

Stalking proudly among his old loves he was heard to say: "Sorry girls, but I'm only a consultant now."

233 A Labourite M.P. likes this best:

An elderly duke was the guest of honor at the annual dinner of his County Conservative Association. The following morning he was walking in the High Street of the county town, and he ran into an old friend who said:

"I'm so sorry I couldn't get to the dinner last night. How was it?"

"Tell you what," said the duke, "let's slip into the club, and you shall buy me a small Madeira and I'll tell you all about the dinner."

Five minutes later they were seated in deep armchairs in the smoking room of the club, each sipping his Madeira and nibbling at a thin biscuit.

"Well, Arthur," said the duke, heaving a deep sigh, "I'll tell you about last night's dinner. If the melon had been as cold as the soup was, and if the soup had been as warm as the claret was, and if the claret had been as old as the chicken was, and if the chicken had been as young as the waitress was, and if the waitress had been as willing as the Duchess was, I'd have had a jolly good evening!"

234 A councilman recounts four tales:

Two old-age Pensioners were reminiscing about their experiences in the Boer War.

First Pensioner to the other: "George, do you remember them pills they used to give us in the Army — you know, them pills which they told us would help us to keep our minds off the girls?"

George: "Aye, come to think of it, I do."

First Pensioner: "Well, do you know I think mine are beginning to work."

111

An Irishman on a visit to Liverpool meets a friend.
The friend: "Hullo, Paddy, when did you come over?"
Paddy: "Yesterday."
The friend: "And did you come by sea or air?"
Paddy: "I don't know, you see my wife bought the tickets."

The vicar was rather taken aback when he noticed that a girl in his congregation bowed her head every time the devil was mentioned, so he stopped her on her way out of the church and asked her why she did it.

The girl replied: "Well, vicar, politeness costs nothing and you never know."

Hikers from Aberdeen, caught by a snowstorm in the Cairngorms, took refuge in a hut for the night.

Next morning a search party with Red Cross personnel set out to find them. They saw the hut and knocked on the door.

Voice from inside: "Who's there?"

"The Red Cross."

Voice from inside: "We've already given, thank you."

235 A judge reports this dilemma:

A wife gives her husband two ties for Christmas and he comes down to breakfast wearing one on Christmas morning.

"Oh, my dear! Didn't you like the other one?"

236 A famous actor and raconteur lives up to his reputation:

A man was lonely and bought a budgerigar on the understanding it would talk to him.

Disappointed by the bird's lack of conversation, he complained to the pet shop proprietor, who advised the purchase of a mirror, and when this failed to make his feathered friend converse, suggested some cuttlefish wedged between the bars.

After this, the man returned daily to the shop equally disappointed, and was advised to buy a swing, and then a ladder, and finally a bell to give the little bird a purpose in life.

"You will find," said the pet shop proprietor, "once he has given himself a swing, loosened his beak with the cuttlefish, climbed the ladder and rung the bell, he is sure to say something."

A week later the man returned triumphant.

"It worked," he said. "He swung, swallowed, climbed, rang the bell and then fell backwards on to the floor of the cage with his feet in the air."

"Did he say anything?"

"Yes, just before he expired he said: 'Did no one tell you about *bird seed*?' "

237 **A Lord of Appeal brings up a case:**

A man became involved in some litigation in the High Court. All his friends told him that as difficult and important points would arise it would be wise for him to obtain legal advice and to be represented at the hearing. He thought otherwise. Without any professional help he conducted his own case.

When he came to his final speech he concluded with an eloquent flourish:

"I am aware, My Lord, that there is an old adage which says that he who is his own lawyer hath a fool for a client: yet such, My Lord, is my respect for this Court that it is with confidence that I leave my case in your hands."

There were reasons which unavoidably prevented him from remaining in Court to hear the judgment. He left some money

with the usher to pay for a telegram which he asked might be sent
to him to tell him the result of the case.

An hour or two later a telegram arrived. With trembling hands
he opened it. It read:

"Old adage affirmed — with costs."

238 **Compliments of a Development Commissioner from Ireland:**

I was presenting the prizes on speech day at an English school.
After the ceremony the boys spontaneously started singing
"When Irish Eyes Are Smiling," obviously as a compliment to
to me. The singing was untuneful, out of key and even raucous.

I noticed a lady in the platform party putting her handkerchief
to her eye, to wipe away a tear. Thinking she had become emo-
tionally overcome, I put my hand on her shoulder and said:

"Are you Irish?"

"No," she replied, "I'm a music teacher."

239 **An Air Vice-Marshal goes through his files:**

The night was clear and starlit as the jumbo jet plowed its way
across the Atlantic at 35,000 feet en route for London Airport.

Two hours or so out from New York the captain spoke on the
intercom:

"I have had to close down No. 1 engine; sorry about this, we
shall be about 20 minutes late at Heathrow."

All was quiet for the next few minutes and the passengers went
on sipping their free drinks in the first-class compartment until
the captain spoke again:

"Sorry everybody, trouble with No. 2 engine; I have had to
shut it down and we shall be about 40 minutes late in London."

Half an hour later more trouble was apparent and the captain,
without the slightest hint of concern in his voice, spoke up again:

"This really is getting embarrassing; No. 3 engine has cut out;
I'm afraid we're going to be a couple of hours late on this run."

The only comment from among the passengers came from an
Irishman as he accepted his seventh whisky from the stewardess:

"Let's hope we don't lose any more engines or we'll be up here
all night!"

240 An actor entertains with this bit:

This after-dinner story was told at a Stage Golfing Society dinner at the Savoy Hotel by an old friend and incomparable raconteur.

He recounted how he had a fire in his bedroom and the insurance company was unwilling to compensate for the damage as it said he had obviously gone to bed drunk and had been smoking and set fire to the bed through carelessness.

His reply was that in the first place he had been stone-cold sober and in the second place the bed was already on fire when he got into it.

241 Cheers for a Lieut.-Colonel:

A young woman at her first cocktail party was overheard to say to her escort:

"I have had only tee martoonis; I'm not so drunk as thinkle peop I am but I fool so feelish and the drunker I sit the longer I get."

242 A landowner likes this sage advice:

A young Irish girl goes to church for confession, and says to the priest:

"Oh Father, Father, I have sinned grievously. On Monday night I slept with Sean. On Tuesday night I slept with Patrick, and on Wednesday night I slept with Mick. Oh Father, Father, what shall I do?"

"My child, my child," replied the priest, "go home and squeeze the juice from a whole lemon and drink it."

"Oh, Father, Father, will this purge me of my sin?" she asked.

"No child, but it will take the smile off your face."

243 From a Commonwealth Governor-General:

I attended a dinner recently where the evils of drink were to be discussed.

The speaker, after the usual anti-drink speech, exemplified his reasons by showing the guests a live worm placed in a glass of water and another live worm put into a glass of whisky and water.

Half an hour later he showed off the two glasses. The worm in the water was wriggling strongly but the worm in the whisky was dead as a door nail.

He turned around to his audience and said:

"Now what is the moral of this demonstration?"

A reply came quickly:

"If you don't care to get worms, drink whisky."

244 An educator contributes this:

A man who unexpectedly gave $100,000 to an appeal was asked how he was able to give so much.

"A little of it," he said, "is due to hard work, a little more to frugal habits, and $98,000 to a recent legacy from a rich uncle."

245 A veterinary professor advises:

The professor was addressing an 8 a.m. lecture.

"I've found that the best way to start the day is to exercise for five minutes, take a deep breath of air and then finish with a cold shower. Then I feel rosy all over."

A sleepy voice from the back of the room:

"Tell us more about Rosy."

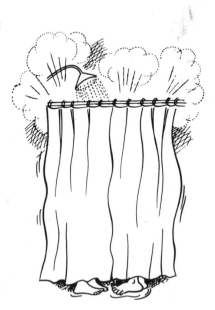

246 **An Irish Prime Minister has a winner:**

A man was very worried about his wife's state of mind, so he went to see a psychiatrist.

The following conversation ensued:

Husband: "The trouble about my wife is that she thinks she is a horse."

Psychiatrist: "I am afraid that if she thinks she's a horse, it will be very expensive to cure her."

Husband: "Have no worry, doctor, have no fear; she's just won the Kentucky Derby!"

247 **A tobacco executive has the last word:**

An Ambassador from an Oriental country in taking leave of Lord Lansdowne said:

"My Lord, I must not cockroach on your time any further."

The diplomatic Lord Lansdowne replied:

"Oh! your Excellency, do not hurry away. Before you go I wish to congratulate you on the command of the English language that you have acquired during your short stay. I am sure your Excellency would not take it amiss, however, if I point out that the correct word is not 'cockroach' but 'encroach'."

"My lord," replied the Ambassador, "forgive me, but I am addressing you and therefore I use the word 'cockroach' whereas if I had been addressing her ladyship I would then be correct to use the word 'hencroach'."

248 **A Professor of Physics tells how to succeed:**

An architect, whose designs were always accepted by the commission in charge of buildings, was asked by a less successful colleague for the secret of his success.

"Very simple," he said. "When I design a building, I put in a prominent place on it two very ugly dogs. When members of the commission object I insist that they are essential for the artistic balance of the design, which would be ruined without them. After prolonged argument I finally agree to remove the dogs, and the commission then passes the design."

117

249 An industrial secretary adds to Churchillian lore:

Sir Winston Churchill (at a diplomatic reception where he was served a very weak whisky and soda):

"My boy, which did you put in first — the whisky or the soda?"

Attendant (anxious to show that he knew what he was doing):

"Oh, sir, I put in the whisky first."

Churchill: "That's very good. Then no doubt I shall come to it in due course!"

And also contributes another:

Small boy: "Grandfather, were you in the Ark?"

Grandfather (very grumpy): "No, I was *not* in the Ark."

Small boy (with relentless logic): "Well, why weren't you drowned then?"

250 An Art School Principal marks his words:

At a marketing conference dinner the talk was about the difficulty of language and communications in international trade.

The director of an engineering firm said that his export director was astonished to receive an order from Russia for a thousand water sheep. A representative was dispatched to investigate.

The actual requirement was for hydraulic rams.

251 A legal writer says it in a nutshell:

An English bishop was making a tour of some schools in a rural district in Africa. He asked a little black boy whether he liked being at school.

"Yes, sir," answered the boy, "because if you haven't got education you've sure got to use your brains."

Another from the same contributor:

An Irishman was giving evidence in an English case, and the judge formed the strong impression that the witness was not telling the truth.

"What happens in your country," the judge asked him, "to a witness who tells lies?"

To which the Irishman replied:

"Sure, your Honor, I think his side usually wins."

252 **A playwright defines diplomacy with this story:**

There's this rich bachelor, who lives alone with a cat which he adores, and is looked after by a faithful manservant.

He goes off on vacation to Cannes leaving the manservant in charge of pussy. On arrival at the hotel he finds a telegram awaiting him which states baldly:

"Pussy dead."

He is deeply shocked, returns to London where he berates his manservant for tactlessness and insensitivity. He says:

"Look, Wilkins, if anything similar should ever occur, you should send a telegram saying: 'Pussy's on the roof and won't come down.' Then wait a few hours before sending a second telegram saying: 'Pussy fell off roof, badly injured.' Then wait a few more hours before sending a third telegram saying: 'Regret pussy is dead.' That way it lessens the shock."

The manservant takes note of this and apologizes.

The next year the man went off on his vacation as usual.

On his arrival at the hotel he found a telegram waiting him which said:

"Your mother's on the roof and won't come down."

253 A well-known entertainer remedies all ills:

This fellow was walking into the doctor's office. He bumped into a very young and pretty girl coming out, but she was sighing and sobbing bitterly.

"Oh, come," he said, "it can't be as bad as all that."

She said: "Oh, but it is, the doctor's just told me that I am pregnant."

The man turned to the doctor and said:

"Is it true?"

The doctor said:

"No, but it's cured her hiccups."

254 A Sheriff of the city overheard this:

The captain instructs the waiter:

"Push the 'plat de jour,' it's yesterday's."

255 More Churchilliana, this one from a Queen's Counsel:

Winston Churchill used to say that there were only two things more difficult than making an after-dinner speech — one was climbing a wall which is leaning towards you and the other, kissing a girl who is leaning away from you.

256 A naval surgeon expresses sentiments:

A proposal to erect a statue to an unpopular local dignitary was very much opposed by the town council with one exception.

The dissenting argument put forward was, although it would afford shelter in bad weather and shade in summer, the pigeons would undoubtedly express the general feeling in a most appropriate way.

257 An Admiral also understands women:

At a cocktail party a feather-brained young woman was talking a lot of nonsense. After she had uttered some particularly outrageous remark her escort remonstrated:

"Darling — don't you *ever* think before you speak?"

Sweetly she replied:

"How can I think before I've heard what I've got to say."

120

258 Compliments of a Colonial Official:

A man was just finishing his lunch in a restaurant. The waitress asked if he would take coffee.

"Yes, please," he replied.

The waitress went off but came back quickly and asked:

"With cream or without, sir?"

"Without cream," he replied.

Then followed a much longer wait before the waitress returned, rather flustered, and said apologetically:

"I'm sorry, sir. There is no more cream. Will you have it without milk?"

259 A government minister lends this handy advice:

This story concerns a large company which required an economic adviser. The managing director decided he needed a well-qualified economist, but it must be someone with only one arm.

A number of candidates were interviewed; many had high qualifications but all were turned down because they had two arms. At last one of them asked him:

"What does it matter? Why do you insist on a one-armed economic adviser?"

"Because I am sick and tired of getting advice which begins 'On the one hand this . . . and on the other hand that . . . .' "

260 A famous author has a golden oldie:

Two men are sitting up late and have been drinking hard. Their talk, which is about anything, wanders to the weight of babies at birth.

First man: "Ol' man, d'you know that when I was born I only weighed $4\frac{1}{2}$ pounds?!"

Second man: "Did you live?"

First man: "Did I live? You ought to see me now!"

261 A Marine Colonel finds this concise enough:

All stories, especially after-dinner ones, should be short and to the point. This was well known to at least one small boy, who, on being asked to write a story in class containing elements of Romance, Royalty, Mystery and Religion, completed the task in thirty seconds.

On being asked by the teacher, he read his story out: "God," said the duchess, "I'm pregnant. Who done it?"

262 A Member of Parliament likes this best:

A speaker said that while changing for dinner his small daughter went into her mother's bathroom and remarked on the size of her tummy.

"Yes, darling, you see daddy has given me a little baby."

After a pause to digest the information the girl rushed into her father's dressing-room:

"Daddy," she cried, "did you give mummy a little baby?"

"Well . . . er . . . yes I did," said father.

"Oh well," said the daughter resignedly, "she's eaten it!"

263 An author remembers this anecdote fondly:

The 11th Duke of St. Albans, with advancing years, decided that he did not like going out to dinner. He preferred his own home.

But there came an occasion when the Duchess bullied him so much that he agreed to go out to dinner — that once. At dinner he sat on his hostess's *left* instead of her right, as he should have been entitled to by rank, for he was positively the only duke present. Not wanting to be out of his own home anyway, he was annoyed. He decided to go to sleep, and being a man of strong character, he . . . slept.

He slept through the soup, the fish and the roast . . . and awoke with a start. Where was he? At all events, there was a lady, on his right hand, staring fixedly at him.

With old-world courtesy, he turned to her:

"Madam," he said, "I'm afraid I don't know who the devil you are. But at least I can apologize for the filthy food here. We've had to fire the cook."

264 **A musician contributes a merry moment in geography:**

Ivan was a very unhappy farmer. His land was on the war-torn Polish/Russian frontier and his citizenship changed constantly from Russian to Polish according to local skirmishes, or national troubles or even international force of arms. This aged him before his time, and he longed for his status to be settled one way or another.

After 50 years of uncertainty a border commission sat; it sat and sat and Ivan grew greyer and more lined. Eventually he heard they'd decided, once and for all. They brought him the news.

Ivan: "Tell me, tell me, what am I finally?"

They: "Ivan, you're to be a Pole."

Ivan: "Thank God. I couldn't have stood another of those Russian winters."

265 **From a broadcaster who speaks from hearsay:**

After-dinner speaking is a technique all its own, and one of the most enjoyable moments for me came when someone was giving his "Reply on behalf of the guests."

The scene was an unusually lavish banquet at one of London's dwindling number of multi-star hotels. Commenting on the wonderful fare provided, the speaker pointed out that in 15th-century Rome, the Best People were those who were able to observe casually:

"Oh, by the way, I'm dining with the Borgias tonight."

They were naturally proud to be invited he said, as we, the guests, were proud in our turn to be present.

The one difference, however, is that none of those 15th-century Top People was ever heard to say:

"Oh, by the way, I dined with the Borgias *last night*. . . ."

266 A diplomat finds the vicar undiplomatic:

An American had been for some time in a Cornish village, trying to trace his ancestry. He had gone through the parish registers, and when it was time for him to leave he called on the vicar to thank him for all the help he had given him. He said he wanted to thank him and give him some money for all the trouble he had taken. The vicar said he really didn't want any reward; it had been a pleasure.

"But surely you must have some need in connection with your church," said the American.

The vicar said that it was true that there were expenses in connection with the church, but they were large; the roof, he said, had got the death-watch beetle and must be renewed.

The American asked how much that would be.

The vicar said it was very costly; the expense might amount to as much as £7,000.

The American said: "Oh, that's about 20,000 dollars. O.K. I'll do it!"

The vicar was overwhelmed with gratitude.

"That," he said, "is most generous. I hardly know how to thank you. When the work is done we shall have a dedication service and we should hope you could come."

The American said it was impossible; he had so much business.

"But," he said, "you could do one thing for me — make a recording of the service and send it to me."

"Very willingly," the vicar said.

The record reached the American and he went into his study to play it, he then burst into the next room raging with anger. His wife asked what was wrong.

"I've been insulted," he said, "they have no gratitude."

She asked just what was wrong, and he said she should come and listen to the play-back.

And so it began:

"Oh, Lord, we thank you for all the blessings you have brought to our church, and above all that wonderful succour (sucker) you sent us from America."

267 **A designer and craftsman copies a gambit:**

My predecessor as Director of the Design Council once found himself at a dinner for a mixed bag of manufacturers and, not knowing the neighbor on his right, asked him what his firm made and got the immediate reply: "Oh, about fifty thousand a year."

In due course I found myself at a similar dinner at Birmingham and, not knowing my neighbor at the table, used the same opening gambit and got an even more surprising answer:

"Oh, we make seventeenth century sundial faces."

When I said I didn't believe it, my neighbor replied:

"Oh yes we do — we bury them for a little while and when we dig them up no one can tell the difference."

268 **An actor-comedian shows why he is famous for after-dinner speaking:**

A certain President of the United States was holding a dinner at The White House. Among the guests was an Indian Chief dressed in full regalia, even to the Crown and Tail of Feathers.

The President seated the First Lady next to the Indian Chief, to make him feel at ease and also because the Chief held 51% of a big oil field.

When the dinner commenced and soup was served, the wife of the President smiled at the Chief and said:

"You like-um soupee?"

The Chief acknowledged the remark with a slight nod of the head.

When the second course was served she said: "You like-um turkey?"

Again the Chief smiled and nodded. This went on through every course.

After coffee, the Chief was called upon to reply for the guests, which he did in a brilliant speech and in faultless English.

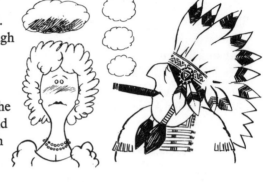

He sat down to a deafening applause, and turning to the President's wife, he said:

"You like-um speechy?"

269 **From a professor of English delving into linguistics:**

At a conference on linguistics, a professor of Spanish was in conversation with a professor of Irish. The Spanish professor asked if in the Irish language there was the equivalent of the Spanish *mañana*.

After pondering for some moments, the Irish professor said:

"Well, yes we have, indeed we have several, but none of them convey the same sense of urgency."

270 **A famous actor can give good advice:**

There was a man who had the fortune to win a prize in a lottery — $5,000 I think it was.

"My goodness, can you believe it?" he asked his wife, " $5,000! Aren't we the luckiest people in the world?"

126

His wife was not quite as elated as he had expected. Indeed frowned a little and then said:

"Oh, yes, but what about all the begging letters?"

"Oh, my dear," he replied happily, "you just keep on writing them."

271 **From an author-playwright setting a scene:**

A constable on a late-night beat which took him through a London West End square noticed a well-dressed man leaning drunkenly up against the front door of one of the houses.

"It's all right, officer," said the man, "I live here."

"Then why not go home?" asked the constable.

"Lost my latch key."

"Then why not ring?"

"Have rung."

"Well, there are lights showing. Why not ring again?"

"No. Let 'em wait!"

272 **This author says it's just a matter of time:**

The speaker had been droning on for an hour and twenty minutes when he suddenly noticed that a number of his listeners' heads were on the tables.

"I am so terribly sorry," he said. "Mr. Chairman, I fear I have gone on far too long. I do apologize to everyone. You see, the trouble is I have no watch with me, and there is no clock in the hall."

And a loud voice came from the far end of the hall:

"There's a calendar on the wall behind you."

273 **An executive recalls a famous witticism:**

Disraeli, when offered the sherbet at a banquet, turned to his neighbor and murmured appreciatively:

"Thank God, something warm at last."

274 **A Commonwealth officer recalls the blackout:**

At Buckie station during the blackout, there was no station name and no lights, and Lady Adam was sitting in a compartment of the train opposite an old fishwife. The porter came down the platform shouting:

"Onybody here for Buckie? Onybody here for Buckie?"

At every shout the fishwife winced and drew herself up. As the train steamed out from the platform, the old girl leaned across and with a confidential smile said:

"Ah'm for Buckie mysel' but I wasna going to tell yon hollerin' devil."

275 **An agriculturist finds fun in the desert:**

A detachment of the French Foreign Legion was trudging across the Sahara; they were hot and sticky, dusty and very depressed.

After a long time the commander called them to a halt and addressed them. He said:

"I have two things to tell you. One of them is good news, the other is not so good and that is the one I'll tell you first. We are absolutely and utterly lost and there's nothing to eat but camel droppings."

The second in command said: "Very well, mon commandant, now please tell us the good news."

The commander said: "Well, there's plenty of it."

276 **From a marine biologist:**

A lady was once asked to lunch by a friend. After they had eaten, her host, who was a keen gardener, asked her if she would like

128

him to show her around his garden. She said that she would be delighted.

So he took her around the garden, of which he was very proud, and spoke about the habits of each plant giving at the same time their full Latin names.

When they had finished their perambulation, she thanked him profusely and said:

"What a clever man you are to remember all those Latin names. I only know two."

"Indeed," he replied, "and which are they?"

"One," she said, "is *Aurora Borealis*, and the other is *delirium tremens*."

277 **A wine expert describes a wedding procession:**

It was a big wedding at a seaside village in the Thirties, and, because of the bride's family's long association with the local lifeboat, the crew had come to line the path from the door of the church to the gate.

It was a rowing and sailing lifeboat, so it was a large crew, splendidly arrayed in oilskins, that raised their oars, shining in the sunlight, to make an archway under which the bridal procession passed.

At the front of the watching crowd was a little girl and her mother. They came from the East End of London, and were on vacation.

As always there was a bit of a hush as the bridge and groom neared the gate, so the little girl was clearly heard to say:

"Mum, aren't them OARS loverly!"

To which Mum was equally clearly heard to reply:

"'Ush! Them aren't 'Ores, them's bridesmaids."

278 **Compliments of a Civil Service Administrator:**

A little girl finds her mother with her face covered with face cream and "beauty" preparations, and asks, "What is that for?" and is told:

"That is to make Mummy beautiful."

And she says: "Then why doesn't it?"

And another from the same person:

A Cambridge don of an older generation had been in the habit of speaking scornfully of some of his younger colleagues whom he feared from time to time were prostituting their vocation by giving talks on the radio.

One day he himself was astonished to receive an invitation to do so, the invitation ending "fee 20 guineas."

The don sent off a telegram accepting, adding:

"Should I send the 20 guineas in advance?"

279 **An Admiral reviews the feet:**

An elderly man complained of a pain in his left leg.

"It's just old age," said the doctor.

"Can't be that," said the patient, "the other leg is the same age, and that don't hurt."

280 **A Lord of Appeal tells this shaggy dog tale:**

A man recently went into a veterinary office and asked that his dog's tail be removed. The veterinary surgeon said:

"It is true that that is an operation which we sometimes perform. But it is most unusual on a dog with a beautiful bushy tail like yours. Why do you want it removed?"

The customer replied: "Well, the truth is that my mother-in-law is coming to stay and I don't want her to get even the smallest sign of welcome."

281 **This Royal Engineer never ducks the issue:**

A man due to appear in a minor lawsuit before a subordinate judge met a pal in a pub the night before. After a few pints and much discussion the friend said:

130

"You'll easily get it settled right. Just send the judge a couple of ducks beforehand."

Next morning the litigant met his solicitor and told him what he intended doing. The solicitor was shocked and said:

"On no account must you do that. We have a pretty weak case anyway, and if you send the judge anything he is bound to rule against you."

When the case came on our friend won.

He took the solicitor over to the pub to celebrate. The solicitor said:

"I am astonished at this result. Frankly, I never thought we had a chance."

The litigant explained that "a couple of ducks" had done it. The solicitor was scandalized:

"Do you really mean to say, after all the warnings I gave you, you sent the judge the ducks?"

"Yes," came the reply, "indeed I did, but I put the other party's name on the label."

282 **Cheers from a Royal Air Force Marshal:**

In the happy old days, the garrison of Aden always included a battalion of British infantry, of which one company was detached for, I think, six months at a time, and formed the garrison of the island of Kamarin, in the Red Sea.

A fresh battalion had recently taken over at Aden, who were not yet familiar with the tropics and their peculiar diseases. And one day they got a signal from their detached company to say:

"We have a case of beri beri here. What should we do with it?"

Next morning, the reply came from battalion:

"Give it to the Sergeants' Mess. They'll drink anything."

283 From a writer who doesn't mince words:

A distinguished English-
man went to New York
with the usual letters of
introduction.

He was met, on a
blazing hot day, by a
leading citizen who took
him to see the sights.
After an exhausting
morning they went to the
top of the Empire State
Building, and on coming
down the host said:

"What can I do for
you now?"

Guest: "All I want to
have now is something
tall and cool and full of
gin."

"Easy, man — just
come around and meet
the wife!"

284 A favorite joke from an Air Vice-Marshal:

An attractive young girl trying to reach the Far East stowed
away on board ship.

After a fortnight or so she was discovered and taken before the
captain.

He was surprised to find her well fed and well turned-out and
asked who among the crew had befriended her. She demurred,
but when pressed finally admitted that she had been to the second
officer's cabin every day for a bath and a meal.

"And what did he want in return?" was the question.

"I suppose you might say he took advantage of me," was her
murmured reply.

"I'll say he did," retorted the captain. "You're on the Liverpool-to-Birkenhead ferry."

285 **The facts of life from a diplomat's viewpoint:**
A small boy, wanting help over a school essay, asked his mother how he came into the world. Unprepared and flustered, she fell back on the stork story, with suitable trimmings.

Looking a little puzzled, he went into the next room and asked Grandma how his mother — and for that matter she herself — had arrived.

His grandmother, who had overheard the first exchange, gave him the same reply with even greater circumstantial detail about the sagacity and accuracy of the stork as a delivery agent.

The boy thanked her politely and went off to write his essay. It began:

"So far as I can make out there has not been a natural birth in my family for three generations."

286 **A prominent radiologist scans the horizon:**
I have in my time had to do a good deal of after-dinner speaking, mostly to medical audiences. I have told very few stories. I have, however, often tried to work into my theme some appropriate or witty sayings to give it point. Here are a few:

Toscanini once said that he kissed his first woman and smoked his first cigarette on the same day and had never had time for tobacco since.

A notice outside a Temperance meeting said: "Alcohol kills slowly." Underneath somebody had written "So who's in a hurry."

Sir Edward Maufe, the celebrated architect, arrived late at a banquet. Wending his way around the table he leant over the shoulder of the president to apologize and said in a whisper, "I'm Maufe," to which the president replied, "Oh dear, I'm so sorry you can't stay."

133

287 **A headmaster on philology:**

There was once an aged charwoman who was describing to a goggling circle of her cronies her husband's last moments.

"And wot were 'is last words, Mrs. Jones?"

"'E didn't 'ave no last words. Oi was with 'im till *the end*."

288 **A hospital director is fond of this one:**

Two senior retired Army officers were chatting in their club about the shortcomings of the modern generation.

"Do you know," said the general, "I was telling my daughter-in-law that my grandfather was killed at Waterloo. She looked up with a sympathetic expression and said: 'Oh, how sad. On what platform did it happen?' "

"Ridiculous," said the brigadier, "as if it mattered what platform he was on."

289 **An Army Colonel does a bit of eavesdropping:**

An old lady got into a railway carriage where two British gentlemen were moaning over their losses at a race track. After a time the old lady got up to get out at a station and as she left the carriage she handed one of the gentlemen a £1 note, saying:

"You are obviously so kind to animals I would like to give you this £1."

"We are not particularly kind to animals," replied the gentleman.

"Oh yes, you are," replied the old lady. "I heard you say you put your shirt on that bleeding animal that was scratched."

290 **From a politician—all the way:**

The Archbishop of Canterbury was visiting a small town parish.

The next day in the street a non-churchgoer asked one of the faithful whether the Archbishop's visit had made an impact.

"Well," came the reply, "I would put it this way. At the end of his sermon there was a great awakening in the congregation."

291 The Lord Mayor of London really likes overseas visitors:

About 2 p.m. one day an American couple were passing Runnymede and saw the sign: "Magna Carta signed here 1215."

Wife to husband: "Oh, George, what a pity. I guess we just missed it."

292 A party leader defines the clerical code:

Lord William Cecil, Bishop of Exeter, was very vague. The wine was poured out for everyone (save an old lady on his left), who was given water.

"Could I have some wine, my Lord Bishop?"

"Apologies — I thought you were a member of the Temperance League."

"Oh, no — a member of the Purity League."

Bishop: "So sorry — I knew there was something you didn't do!"

293 A political service official likes animals:

A vet went to a farm to perform artificial insemination of a cow. As he approached the cow he asked the cowman if she was quiet.

"Oh yes," he was answered.

As the vet ran his hand along her back towards the rear, the cow gave him an awful side kick.

"Oh, I thought you said she was quiet."

The old cowman looked puzzled and surprised as he scratched his head. Then light broke over his face.

"Ah," he said, "I guess she ain't seen a bull in a bowler hat afore!"

294 A college officer resurrects a life saver:

During the Nazi occupation of Norway two friends were sitting in the park in Oslo and a passing Gestapo official overheard one say to the other:

"You know, there's only one man responsible for this horrible war."

The speaker was at once arrested and marched off to police headquarters. Here he was asked to repeat his remark.

"Certainly," says he, "I said that there was only one man responsible for this horrible war."

"And who is that man?"

"Why, Winston Churchill, of course."

The interrogator, somewhat taken aback, said:

"Yes, um, yes, of course, and you are right. You may take your hat and go."

At the door the Norwegian turned, paused and looked back and asked:

"By the way, who did you think it was?"

295 An Air Force Commander on medical practice:

A fat man went to his doctor to see if he could do anything about his obesity. He was given pills to be taken every night for two months with a promise of a loss of 28 pounds or more.

The first night he took the pill and dreamed the most marvelous dream, being on a beautiful island, inhabited by the most gorgeous girls — all naked — whom he proceeded to chase around the island. The result was a pound gone in the morning.

This happened every night for two months and the 28 pounds were dutifully lost.

Another man, equally fat, asked him how he had done it. Off he went to the same doctor for the same prescription — but his dreams were of a rocky island on which *he* was chased every night by horrible creatures, but the result was the same — 28 pounds lost.

He went to the doctor to ask why he had such horrible dreams and the first man such good ones. The doctor's reply was:

"Oh well, you see, he was a private patient!"

296 **An industrialist features respect for your elders:**

Patrick from Dublin was crossing St. Peter's Square on a wet and gusty evening, his collar turned up against the wind. Suddenly, he clutched at his chest and collapsed in a puddle on the ground.

Providentially, friends were close at hand and immediately rushed to his aid.

"Quick," said Patrick, "get me a rabbi."

"But, Patrick, you're a good Catholic."

"Ah sure, sure," was the reply, "but I wouldn't dream of bringing His Holiness out on a night like this!"

297 **A Judge chalks up one for domestic felicity:**

A secretary agreed to work late with her boss and when they had finished work offered to drop him off at his home in her car.

On the way he offered to buy her a meal, which she accepted. They also had a couple of bottles of wine and quite spontaneously, for they were not having an affair, ended up in her flat and in bed. Time passed quickly and too late they realized that his wife would need, for that hour, an extremely good explanation for his lateness.

He asked his secretary for, and got, a piece of chalk. Arriving home, his irate wife was waiting.

"And where do you think you've been?"

"Well, actually," he replied, "I was working late with my secretary, I took her for a meal, one thing led to another and we ended up in bed in her flat."

The wife screamed: "You liar. You've been playing darts with the boys. You've still got the piece of chalk behind your ear."

298 **A union official sweetens the insults:**
After a very happy and successful meeting, the secretary asked the chief speaker: "What are your expenses?"

"Nothing," the speaker answered.

"Are you quite sure?" asked the secretary.

"Certain," said the speaker. "I have no expenses."

"Thank you very much," said the secretary. "We have a number of gentlemen who kindly refuse to accept any expenses, and the money we save we put into a special fund so that we will be able to afford to invite better speakers in the future."

299 **A politician on Scots and waste:**
The Scots are reputed to be mean. This is a mistake. They are only careful and hate waste.

An illustration of this is the story of a tourist in a train in the Highlands discovering he wanted to smoke, turning to the Scot who was the other passenger to ask if he could have a match.

"Oh, certainly," said the Scot, carefully taking one match out of his box.

But when the tourist discovered that he had forgotten his cigarettes and dolefully confessed his trouble to the Scot, the latter thereupon extended his hand to the tourist saying:

"Well, you'll no' be needing the match."

300 **A racing official offers a pep talk:**
There was a member of the House of Lords who suspected that a trainer had been doping. So, for months, whenever the trainer had a horse running, his lordship was there watching every movement. There came a day when the trainer had a filly which was not much favored and, after he saddled her, his lordship noticed the trainer take a little box from his pocket, take something out, and gave it to the filly, to swallow. His lordship pounced.

"What's that?"

"Oh, my lord," said the trainer, "it's just a little sweetmeat — nothing at all. I'll have one and you have one."

138

The trainer swallowed the tablet and his lordship found himself doing the same.

A few moments later the jockey came into the ring and the trainer said:

"Take her down very quietly, jump her off, lie on the rails — about fourth — and when you come to the straight, pull her out and go on and win. If anything passes you it will either be his lordship or me."

301 **Grade A logic from a trade union official:**

Some years ago, when I was a weaver, a fellow worker asked me if I proposed to go to the wedding of a mutual friend.

"No," I said, "I haven't been invited."

"Well," he said, "neither have I, but I haven't been told to stay away."

302 **An American story from a British Air marshal:**

A professor of Yale University was an after-dinner speaker at an academic banquet in England.

"As you know," he began, "I come from Yale, and I want to frame my speech around those four letters." His listeners looked hopeful.

"Y," said he, "stands for Youth: our society is a young one. . . ." and he talked about Youth for fifteen minutes.

"Now A," he said, "is for Ambition, the great American virtue . . . ." The guests settled down as he spoke for twenty minutes on Ambition.

"L stands for Learning," he declaimed; and gave fifteen more minutes to Learning.

"And E for that great institution, Education . . . ." His listeners now low in their chairs, he wound up with twenty minutes on Education. As he sat down, he eagerly asked his neighbor, whose eyes were glazing over: "How did I do?"

"I enjoyed it very much," was the faint reply, "and I'm so glad that you're not from Massachusetts Institute of Technology."

303 A judge advocate offers proof positive:

We live in an age in which we are deluged by statistics. The trouble about statistics, however, is that they can be used to prove practically anything at all, and in the last analysis they mean so little.

Every time I see a set of statistics produced to support a particular proposition I always recall a definition I once heard of a statistician.

He is a person who can lie with his head in the icebox and his feet in the oven and be able to say that, on the whole, he was feeling quite normal.

Appendix

The main objectives of Oxfam are to fight hunger and adversity in those parts of the world where even the basic necessities of life are in short supply. Oxfam is a channel for help—from people to people.

Started in 1942 with the concern of a group in Oxford for the starving people of wartorn Greece, it has tried since to respond in a practical way to human need. Today it helps about a thousand projects in over 80 countries.

Oxfam is equipped to rush medical teams and supplies to disaster areas. But more than two-thirds of its funds now go to long-term development schemes—agricultural, medical and training programs. These projects overseas are carried out by the most appropriate local group under the overall supervision of Oxfam's highly experienced field staff, working from 6 bases in Africa, 3 in Latin America, and 6 in Asia.

All this work is made possible by the voluntary help and gifts of thousands of supporters. A book of after-dinner stories may appear to be far removed from Oxfam's objectives and yet the generous donors of the stories contained in this book—and many others whose stories could not be included—have contributed more than money to the cause. Because all the royalties have been donated to Oxfam, this book will not only bring laughter and enjoyment to its readers but every copy sold will help the work of Oxfam.

It has often been said that laughter is a cure for all ills. This book will also help to relieve hunger and hardship.

The Oxfam headquarters are located at 274 Banbury Road, Oxford, England, and the director is Brian W. Walker.

Here are the contributors whose stories were used:

Contributors

1 Lord Aberconway, Industrialist; High Sheriff of Denbighshire, 1950.

2 Lord Abinger, D.L., Farmer and Company Director.

3 Harold Abrahams, C.B.E., M.A., LL.B., Olympic Games Athlete, Author and Broadcaster.

4 Sir John Ackroyd, Bt., Consultant and Investment Adviser to Middle East Companies.

5 The Rev. Professor Peter Ackroyd, M.A., Ph.D., D.D., M.Th., Professor of Old Testament Studies, University of London, since 1961.

6 Air Vice-Marshal Alexander Adams, C.B., D.F.C., Director, The Mental Health Foundation, since 1970.

7 Professor John Frank Adams, M.A., Ph.D., F.R.S., Professor of Astronomy and Geometry, University of Cambridge, since 1970.

8 Sir Godfrey Agnew, K.C.V.O., C.B., Clerk of the Privy Council, 1953–74.

9 Lawrence Airey, Deputy Secretary, H.M. Treasury, since 1973.

10 Sir Geoffrey Aldington, K.B.E., C.M.G., H.M. Ambassador to Luxembourg, 1961–66.

11 Captain John Steele Allan, C.B.E., Company Director.

12 Sir Douglas Allen, G.C.B., F.B.I.M., Permanent Secretary to the Treasury, 1968–74.

13 Sir Philip Allen, G.C.B., Member, Security Commission, since 1973.

14 Rear-Admiral Courtney Anderson, C.B., Flag Officer, Admiralty Interview Board, 1969–71.

15 Sir Eric Ansorge, C.S.I., C.I.E., Indian Civil Service, 1910–46.

16 Sir John Arbuthnot, Bt., M.B.E., T.D., A Church Commissioner for England, since 1962.

17 The Viscount of Arbuthnott, D.S.C., President of the Scottish Landowners' Federation; Landowner and Farmer.

18 Peter Archer, Q.C., M.P., Solicitor-General, since 1974.

19 Professor Sir Alfred Ayer, F.B.A., Professor of Logic in the University of Oxford, since 1959.

20 Lord Aylestone, C.H., C.B.E., Chairman, Independent Broadcasting Authority, 1967–75.

21 Sir Vahé Bairamian, Editor of Publications on Law; Justice, Supreme Court of Nigeria, 1960-68.

22 Sir John Balfour, G.C.M.G., G.B.E., British Ambassador to Argentina, 1948–51, and Spain, 1951–54.

23 Sir Joseph Balmer, J.P., Lord Mayor of Birmingham, 1954–55.

24 Lord Barber, P.C., Chancellor of the Exchequer, 1970–74.

25 The Rt. Rev. C. K. N. Bardsley, C.B.E., D.D., Formerly Bishop of Coventry.

26 Sir Robert Barlow, Industrialist.

142

27 Sir Henry Barnard, Judge of the High Court of Justice, 1944–59; Admiralty Judge of the Cinque Ports.

28 Sir Cecil Bateman, K.B.E., Retired Civil Servant; Director of Allied Irish Banks.

29 Lord Beaumont of Whitley, M.A., President of the Liberal Party, 1969–70.

30 Leslie Herbert Bedford, C.B.E., Formerly Director of Engineering, Guided Weapons Division, British Aircraft Corporation.

31 The Hon. Sir George Bellew, K.C.B., K.C.V.O., F.S.A. Garter Principal King of Arms, 1950–61; Secretary of the Order of the Garter, 1961–74.

32 Sir Robert Bellinger, G.B.E., Lord Mayor of London, 1966–67; Governor, B.B.C., 1968–71.

33 Eric Raymond Bevington, C.M.G., H.M. Colonial Administrative Service, 1935–62.

34 John Benjamin Biddy, Chairman, J. Biddy & Sons Ltd.

35 Lord Birdwood, Executive Search Consultant.

36 Professor John Howard Birkinshaw, D.Sc., F.R.I.C., Emeritus Professor of Biochemistry, University of London.

37 Sir Cyril Black, D.L., J.P., Member of Parliament for Wimbledon, 1950–70.

39 Rt. Hon. David Bleakley, M.A., Northern Ireland Politician; Educationalist and Broadcaster.

38 Sir Adrian Boult, C.H., M.A., D.Mus., Composer and Conductor; Vice-President, Council of the Royal College of Music, since 1963.

40 Brigadier Sir John Boyd, O.B.E., F.R.S., M.D., F.R.C.P., D.P.H., Member, Colonial Medical Research Committee, 1945–60; Chairman, Research Defence Society, 1956–68.

41 Lord Boyd-Carpenter, P.C., D.L., Chairman, Civil Aviation Authority, since 1972.

42 Marshal of the Royal Air Force Sir Dermot Boyle, G.C.B., K.C.V.O., K.B.E., A.F.C., Chief of Air Staff, 1956–59; Vice-Chairman, British Aircraft Corporation, 1962–71.

43 Lord Brabourne, Film and Television Producer.

44 The Marquess of Bristol, Landowner and Industrialist; Hereditary High Steward of the Liberty of St. Edmund.

45 Rabbi Sir Israel Brodie, K.B.E., Chief Rabbi of the United Hebrew Congregations of the British Commonwealth of Nations, 1948–65.

46 Sir Paul Bryan, D.S.O., M.C., M.P., Minister of State, Department of Employment, 1970–72.

47 Captain David Buchan of Auchmacoy, J.P., Member of the London Stock Exchange.

48 Sir Matt Busby, C.B.E., K.C.S.G., Director, Manchester United Football Club, since 1971.

49 Colonel Sir Thomas Pierce Butler, Bt., C.V.O., D.S.O., O.B.E., Resident Governor, Tower of London, 1961–71; Keeper of Jewel House, 1968–71.

50 Sir Sydney Caffyn, C.B.E., Member, Industrial Court, 1959–71.

51 The Rt. Hon. Sir David Cairns, A Lord Justice of Appeal.

52 Montague Calman, F.R.S.A., M.J.I., Scriptwriter.

53 Wyn Calvin, Television Artiste.

54 Lord Campbell of Eskan, Chairman: Commonwealth Sugar Exporters' Association; Milton Keynes Development Corporation; Statesman and Nation Publishing Company.

55 The Archibishop of Canterbury (The Most Rev. and Rt. Hon Donald Coggan, M.A., D.D.).

56 Sir Olaf Caroe, K.C.S.I., Governor, North-West Frontier, 1946–47.

57 The Late Sir Michael Cary, K.C.B., Formerly Permanent Under-Secretary of State, Ministry of Defence.

58 Sir Hugh Casson, P.R.A., R.D.I., Professor, Environmental Design, Royal College of Art, 1952–75.

59 Sir Richard Catling, C.M.G., O.B.E., K.P.M., Commissioner of Police, Kenya, Inspector-General, 1963–64.

60 Sir Charles Cawley, C.B.E., Chief Scientist, Ministry of Power, 1959–67; Civil Service Commissioner, 1967–69.

61 Lord Champion, Deputy Speaker and Deputy Chairman of Committees, House of Lords, since 1967.

62 Viscount Charlemont, Air Ministry Liaison Officer, 8th and 9th U.S. Army Air Force, 1942–45.

63 Lord Clifford of Chudleigh, O.B.E., D.L., Count of the Holy Roman Empire; Farmer and Landowner.

64 Sir Andrew Clark, Bt., M.B.E., M.C., Q.C.

65 Sir Joseph Cleary, J.P., Lord Mayor of Liverpool, 1949–50; Freeman, City of Liverpool, 1970.

66 G. Clouston, Musical Director.

67 Sir Jack Cohen, O.B.E., J.P., Mayor of Sunderland, 1949–50.

68 Air Vice-Marshal Sir John Cordingley, K.C.B., K.C.V.O., C.B.E., Controller, Royal Air Force Benevolent Fund, 1947–62.

69 Lieut.-General Sir John Cowley, G.C., K.B.E., C.B.

70 Sir Beresford Craddock, Barrister; Member of Speaker's Panel of Chairmen, 1966–70.

71 Brigadier Sir Douglas Crawford, C.B., D.S.O., T.D., Lord Lieutenant, Metropolitan County of Merseyside, since 1974.

72 Sir James Currie, K.B.E., C.M.G., H.M. Diplomatic Service until 1967; Community Relations Commission, since 1970.

73 Vice-Admiral Sir John Cuthbert, K.B.E., C.B., Flag Officer Scotland, 1956–58.

74 Professor David Daiches, M.A., D.Phil., L.H.D., F.R.S.L., Professor of English, University of Sussex, since 1961.

75 Lionel Dakers, B.Mus., F.R.A.M., F.R.C.O.(CHM), A.D.C.M., F.R.S.C.M., Director, Royal School of Church Music, since 1972.

76 Tam Dalyell, M.P., P.P.S. to the late R.H.S. Crossman, 1963–70; Vice-Chairman, Parliamentary Labour Party, 1974–76; Member of European Parliament.

77 Colonel D. J. Dean, V.C., O.B.E., Deputy Lieutenant of Kent, 1957.

78 Lord Delfont, Chairman and Chief Executive of Film and Theatre Corporation.

79 Sir Lionel Denny, G.B.E., M.C., Lord Mayor of London, 1965–66.

80 The Duke of Devonshire, M.C., President of the Royal Hospital and Home for Incurables.

84 Peter Dimmock, C.V.O., O.B.E., General Manager, B.B.C. Radio and Television Enterprises, since 1972.

81 Sir Douglas Dodds-Parker, M.A., Member of the European Parliament.

82 Robert Dougall, M.B.E., Freelance Broadcaster, Television and Radio; Author; President, Royal Society Protection of Birds, 1970–75.

83 Judge The Lord Dunboyne.

85 The Bishop of Durham (The Rt. Rev. John Stapylton Habgood, M.A., Ph.D.), Bishop of Durham, since 1973.

86 Sir Cyril Dyson, President of the National Association of Goldsmiths in Great Britain and Ireland, 1957–70.

87 Sir John Eardley-Wilmot, Bt., M.V.O., D.S.C., On the Staff of the Monopolies Commission, since 1967.

88 Viscount Ebrington, Landowner; Late Coldstream Guards.

89 Judge T. Elder-Jones, A Circuit Judge, formerly Judge of County Courts.

90 Air Marshal Sir Thomas Elmhirst, K.B.E., C.B., A.F.C., Lieutenant-Governor and Commander-in-Chief of Guernsey, 1953–58.

91 George Elrick, F.R.S.A., President of the Entertainments Agents Association.

92 Sir John Elstub, C.B.E., Industrialist and Company Director.

93 Lord Erskine of Rerrick, G.B.E., K.St.J., F.R.S.(E), Hon. F.R.C.P.(E), D.L., J.P., Governor of Northern Ireland, 1964–68.

94 Lieut.-General Sir Geoffrey Evans, K.B.E., C.B., D.S.O., General Officer Commanding-in-Chief, Northern Command, 1953–57.

95 Major-General Sir Robert Ewbank, K.B.E., C.B., D.S.O., Commandant, Royal Military College of Science, 1961–64.

96 Sir James Falconer, M.B.E., Town Clerk of Glasgow, 1965-75.

97 The Late Lord Feather, C.B.E., General Secretary, Trades Union Congress, 1969–73.

98 Lord Ferrier, E.D., D.L., Late Chairman of Companies in India and the U.K.; Hon. A.D.C. to Governor of Bombay.

99 Professor David John Finney, M.A., Ph.D., F.R.S., F.R.S.E., Professor of Statistics, University of Edinburgh, since 1966.

100 Viscount FitzHarris.

101 The Rt. Hon. Sir Geoffrey de Freitas, K.C.M.G., M.P., Vice-President of the European Parliament, 1975–76.

102 Sir Geoffrey Furlonge, K.B.E., C.M.G., Author; H.M. Ambassador to Ethiopia 1956–59.

103 Air Vice-Marshal Jack Furner, C.B.E., D.F.C., A.F.C., F.I.P.M., Assistant Air Secretary, Ministry of Defence (Air), 1973–76.

104 Air Vice-Marshal Maxwell Gardham, C.B., C.B.E., Registrar, Ashridge College, Berkhamsted.

105 Lord Gardiner, C.H., P.C., Lord High Chancellor of Great Britain, 1964–70; Chancellor, The Open University, since 1973.

106 Sir Peter Garran, K.C.M.G., H.M. Ambassador to the Netherlands, 1964–70.

107 Peter W. Gibbings, Chairman of The Guardian and Manchester Evening News Ltd.

108 Sir Derek Gilbey, Bt., Retired Wine Merchant.

109 Professor Iain E. Gillespie, M.D., M.Sc., F.R.C.S., Professor of Surgery, University of Manchester, since 1970.

110 Lord Gisborough, D.L., Landowner and Farmer.

111 The Bishop of Gloucester (The Rt. Rev. John Yates, M.A.), Bishop of Gloucester, since 1975.

112 Sir Edward Goad, K.C.M.G., Secretary-General, Inter-Governmental Maritime Consultative Organisation, 1968–73.

113 Lord Adam Gordon, K.C.V.O., M.B.E., Comptroller to Her Majesty Queen Elizabeth The Queen Mother, 1953–73.

114 Major-General R. Gordon-Finlayson, O.B.E., J.P., D.L., President of Nottingham Royal British Legion since 1971; High Sheriff of Nottinghamshire, 1974.

115 Lord Gore-Booth, G.C.M.G., K.C.V.O., Head of Diplomatic Service, 1968–69; Chairman, Save the Children Fund, since 1970.

116 Captain Lord Alastair Graham, Late Royal Navy; Farmer; Former Alderman, East Suffolk County Council.

117 Lord Greenwood of Rossendale, P.C., J.P., D.L. Minister of Housing and Local Government, 1966–70; Pro-Chancellor, University of Lancaster, since 1972.

118 Joseph Greig, Actor.

119 Lord Grenfell, C.B.E., T.D., Deputy Chairman of Committees, House of Lords.

120 Sir Kenneth Grubb, K.C.M.G., President, Church Missionary Society, 1944–69.

121 General Sir John Hackett, G.C.B., C.B.E., D.S.O., M.C., Principal of King's College, London, 1968–75.

122 Archibald Richard Burdon Haldane, C.B.E., D.Litt., Author; Trustee, National Library of Scotland.

123 Sir John Hall, O.B.E., T.D., M.P., Chairman of the Select Committee on Nationalised Industries, 1972.

124 Professor Peter Hall, M.A., Ph.D., F.R.G.S., Professor of Geography, University of Reading, since 1968.

125 John Hannam, M.P., Member of Parliament for Exeter, since 1970.

126 Air Chief Marshal Sir Donald Hardman, G.B.E., K.C.B., D.F.C., Member of Air Council, 1954–58.

127 Sir James Harford, K.B.E., C.M.G., Governor and Commander-in-Chief, St. Helena, 1954–58.

128 Lord Harris, C.B.E., M.C., J.P., Vice-Lieutenant of Kent, 1948–72.

131 The Earl of Harrowby.

129 Sir Charles Hartwell, C.M.G., H.M. Colonial Service, 1927–60.

130 Eric Hartwell, Vice-Chairman and Joint Chief Executive, Trust Houses Forte Ltd.

133 Lieut.-Colonel Harvey Harvey-Jamieson, O.B.E., D.L., Member of The Queen's Bodyguard for Scotland (Royal Company of Archers).

132 Sir Geoffrey Haworth, Bt., M.A., J.P., F.R.S.A., Farmer; Chairman, Halle Concerts Society.

134 Sir Claude Hayes, K.C.M.G., M.A., B.Litt., Chairman, Crown Agents for Overseas Governments and Administrations, 1968–74.

135 Barney Hayhoe, M.P., Opposition Spokesman on Employment, since 1974.

136 The Right Hon. Denis Healey, M.B.E., M.P., Chancellor of the Exchequer, since 1974.

137 Brigadier Simon Heathcote, C.B.E., Chief of Staff, Middle East Command, 1962–64.

138 Sir John Hedges, C.B.E., Solicitor; Chairman, Berkshire Area Health Authority.

139 Sir James Henderson, K.B.E., C.M.G., H.M. Ambassador to Bolivia, 1956–60.

140 Air Chief Marshal Sir Anthony Heward, K.C.B., O.B.E., D.F.C., A.F.C., Air Member for Supply and Organisation, Ministry of Defence, 1973–76.

141 Derek Heys, C.B.E., T.D., Consul for Belgium in Liverpool, since 1966.

142 Sir William Hildred, C.B., O.B.E., Director-General, International Air Transport Association, 1946–66.

143 Sir Austin Bradford Hill, C.B.E., Ph.D., D.Sc., F.R.S., Emeritus Professor of Medical Statistics, London School of Hygiene and Tropical Medicine, University of London.

144 Admiral of the Fleet, Sir Peter Hill-Norton, G.C.B., Chief of the Defence Staff, 1971–73; Chairman, Military Committee of N.A.T.O., since 1974.

145 Sir Frederick Hoare, Bt., Banker; Lord Mayor of London, 1961–62.

146 Sir Julian Hodge, LL.D., Merchant Banker.

147 Brian Harry Holbeche, C.B.E., M.A., Headmaster, King Edward's School, Bath, since 1962; President, Headmasters' Association, 1970.

148 Lord Home of the Hirsel, K.T., D.L., British Prime Minister, 1963–64.

149 Admiral Sir Frank Hopkins, K.C.B., D.S.O., D.S.C., Commander-in-Chief Portsmouth, 1966–67.

151 Lord Horder, Publisher, Composer and Author.

150 Michael Hordern, C.B.E., Actor: Stage, Films, Radio and Television.

152 Major-General Derek Horsford, C.B.E., D.S.O.

153 Jack Howarth, Stage and Television Actor.

154 Lord Howick of Glendale, Merchant Banker; Member of Executive Committee, National Art Collections Fund, since 1973.

155 The Rt. Hon. Cledwyn Hughes, M.P., Chairman of the Parliamentary Labour Party and former Secretary of State for Wales and Minister of Agriculture.

156 Field Marshal Sir Richard Hull, G.C.B., D.S.O., Chief of the Defence Staff, 1965–67; Constable of H.M. Tower of London 1970–75.

157 Christmas Humphreys, Q.C., A Permanent Judge of the Central Criminal Court, 1968–76.

158 Sir Olliver Humphreys, C.B.E., B.Sc., F.Inst.P., F.I.E.E., Founder Chairman, Conference of the Electronics Industry, 1963–67.

159 John Leonard Hunt, M.P., U.K. Representative at the Council of Europe and Western European Union, since 1974.

160 Sir Peter Hutchison, Bt., Clerk of the Peace and County Solicitor, East Suffolk, 1970–72.

161 Fergus Munro Innes, C.I.E., C.B.E., Chairman, India General Navigation and Railway Company, since 1973.

162 Stephen Jack, F.R.S.A., Actor.

163 Hector Beaumont Jacks, M.A., Headmaster, Bedales School, 1946–62.

164 Francis Jackson, Organist and Master of the Music, York Minster.

165 Tom Jackson, General Secretary, Union of Post Office Workers, since 1967.

166 Gordon Jacob, C.B.E., D.Mus., F.R.C.M., Hon. R.A.M., Composer and Conductor; Professor of Theory, Composition and Orchestration, Royal College of Music, 1924–66.

167 Arthur David Jacobs, M.A., Professor, Royal Academy of Music, since 1964; Editor, British Music Yearbook, since 1971.

168 The Hon. Greville Janner, Q.C., M.P., Author and Journalist.

169 Sir Clifford Jarrett, K.B.E., C.B., Chairman, Tobacco Research Council, since 1971.

170 Clive Jenkins, General Secretary, Association of Scientific, Technical and Managerial Staffs.

171 Hugh Jenkins, M.P., Politician, Broadcaster and Lecturer; Minister for the Arts, 1974–76.

172 Leslie Westover Jenkins, C.B.E., Chairman, Forestry Commission, 1965–70.

173 Owen Jennings, R.W.S., R.E., A.R.C.A., F.R.S.A., Artist; Principal, School of Art, Tunbridge Wells, 1934–65.

174 Percival Henry Jennings, C.B.E., Director-General, Overseas Audit Service, 1960–63.

175 Sir Maynard Jenour, T.D., J.P., Industrialist; Vice-Lord Lieutenant of Monmouthshire.

176 Sir George Jessel, Bt., M.C., President, Imperial Continental Gas Association.

177 Sir Richard Hugh Jessel, Member of Advisory Council, Export Credits Guarantee Department, 1950–60.

178 Sir Ronald Johnson, C.B., J.P., Secretary of Commissions for Scotland.

179 (The second story is submitted in memory of the late Sir Duncan Weatherstone, Lord Provost of Edinburgh about 12 years ago, whose favorite story it was.)

180 Hugh R. Jolly, M.A., M.D., F.R.C.P., Physician-in-Charge, Department of Paediatrics, Charing Cross Hospital, since 1965.

181 Sir Glyn Jones, G.C.M.G., M.B.E., Diplomat; Governor-General of Malawi, 1964–66.

182 Frank Judd, M.P., Parliamentary Under-Secretary of State for Defence for the Royal Navy, 1974–76; Parliamentary Under-Secretary of State at the Overseas Development Ministry, since 1976.

183 Dr. Ernest Kay, Journalist and Publisher.

184 Alexander James Kellar, C.M.G., O.B.E., Attached War Office, 1941–65; English Tourist Board, 1970–73.

185 Louis Kentner, Concert Pianist and Composer.

186 Lord Kincraig, Q.C., Senator of the College of Justice in Scotland, since 1972.

187 Lord Kindersley, C.B.E., M.C., Director, Bank of England, 1947–67.

188 Judge Michael King, M.A., A Circuit Judge; Weekend Sailor.

189 The Rev. Professor James Kinsley, M.A., Ph.D., D.Litt., F.B.A., Professor of English Studies, University of Nottingham, since 1961.

190 Sir Norman Kipping, G.C.M.G., K.B.E., Director-General, Federation of British Industries, 1946–65.

191 Air Vice-Marshal George ("Larry") Lamb, C.B.E., A.F.C., Chief of Staff, Headquarters No.18 Group, Royal Air Force, since 1975; International Rugby Referee.

192 Sir Lionel Lamb, K.C.M.G., O.B.E., Diplomat; H.M. Ambassador to Switzerland, 1953–58.

193 Sir John Lang, G.C.B., Secretary of the Admiralty, 1947–61; Principal Adviser on Sport to the Government, 1964–71.

194 Sir Christopher Lawrence-Jones, Bt., M.A., M.B., B.Chir., D.I.H., Industrial Medical Adviser.

195 Judge Paul Layton, A Circuit Judge; Formerly Deputy Chairman, Inner London Quarter Sessions.

196 The Bishop of Leeds (The Rt. Rev. William Gordon Wheeler, M.A.), Roman Catholic Bishop of Leeds, since 1966.

197 The Late Henry Cecil Leon, M.C. (Pseudonym, Henry Cecil), Author; Formerly County Court Judge.

198 Major-General Peter Leuchars, C.B.E., General Officer Commanding Wales, 1973-76.

199 Sir Percy Lister, D.L., Engineer and Industrialist.

200 Sir David Llewellyn, Author, Journalist and Book Reviewer.

201 Judge David Lloyd-Jones, V.R.D., A Circuit Judge.

202 Sir Thomas Lodge, M.B., Ch.B., F.F.R., F.R.C.P., F.R.C.S., Consultant Radiologist, United Sheffield Hospitals, 1946–74.

203 Sir Norman Longley, C.B.E., D.L., Building Contractor; President, International Federation of Building and Public Works Contractors, 1955–57.

204 Judge Allister Lonsdale, A Circuit Judge.

205 The Hon. Ivor Lucas, Diplomat; Head of Middle East Department, Foreign and Commonwealth Office, since 1975.

206 Sir Robert Lusty, Publisher; A Governor of the B.B.C., 1960–68.

207 Sir Patrick McCall, M.B.E., T.D., D.L., Member of the Economic Social Committee of the E.E.C.

208 Sir Peter Macdonald, D.L., W.S., Industrialist.

209 Air Vice-Marshal D. M. T. Macdonald, C.B., Director-General of Manning, Air Ministry, 1958–61.

210 Professor Gordon Peter McGregor, B.A., M.Ed., Professor of Education, University of Zambia, 1970; Principal, Bishop Otter College, Chichester, since 1970.

211 Sir Hamish MacLaren, K.B.E., C.B., D.F.C., Director of Electrical Engineering, Admiralty, 1945–60.

212 Judge John MacManus, T.D., Q.C., A Circuit Judge, since 1971.

213 Lord Macpherson of Drumochter, F.R.S.A., F.R.E.S., F.Z.S., Banker; Chief of the Scottish Clans Association of London, 1972–74.

214 Sir Patrick Macrory, Barrister and Author; Director, Bank of Ireland Group, since 1971.

215 Major-General Reginald W. Madoc, C.B., D.S.O., O.B.E., Royal Marines (Retired).

216 Magnus Magnusson, Writer and Broadcaster.

217 Sir George Mallaby, K.C.M.G., O.B.E., Diplomat; High Commissioner for the United Kingdom in New Zealand, 1957–59.

218 Colonel Sir Stuart Mallinson, C.B.E., D.S.O., M.C., D.L., Deputy Lieutenant Greater London, 1966.

219 Professor Sir William Mansfield Cooper, LL.M., Professor of Industrial Law, University of Manchester, 1949–70; Vice-Chancellor, University of Manchester, 1956–70.

220 Sir James Marjoribanks, K.C.M.G., Chairman, E.E.C. Committee of Scottish Council (Development and Industry), since 1971.

221 Judge John Fitzgerald Marnan, M.B.E., A Circuit Judge, since 1972.

222 Sir Ralph Marnham, K.C.V.O., M.Chir., F.R.C.S., Serjeant Surgeon to The Queen, 1967–71.

223 Lord Marples, P.C., Postmaster-General, 1957–59; Minister of Transport, 1959–64.

224 Sir Alan Marre, K.C.B., Parliamentary Commissioner for Administration, since 1971.

150

225 Sir Frank Marshall, M.A., LL.B., Chairman, Maplin Development Authority, 1973–74.

226 Roy Mason, M.P., Member of Parliament for Barnsley; Secretary of State for Defence, since 1974.

227 Professor Leonard Maunder, B.Sc., Ph.D., Sc.D., C.Eng., F.I.Mech.E., Professor of Mechanical Engineering, University of Newcastle-upon-Tyne, since 1967.

228 Lord Maybray-King, P.C., Speaker of the House of Commons, 1965–71; Deputy Speaker of the House of Lords, since 1971.

229 Sir Peter Medawar, C.H., F.R.S., Nobel Laureate in Medicine, 1960.

230 S thony Meyer, M.P., Politician and Diplomat.

231 Ci Michelmore, C.B.E., Television Broadcaster and Producer.

232 Sir George Middleton, K.C.M.G., F.R.S.A., Diplomat; H.M. Ambassador to the United Arab Republic, 1964–66.

233 Ian Mikardo, M.P., Chairman, International Committee of the Labour Party, since 1974.

234 Sir Richard Millar, M.A., Chairman, Arthritis and Rheumatism Council, North-West Region.

235 The Hon. Sir Alan Mocatta, O.B.E., Judge of the High Court of Justice (Queen's Bench Division), since 1961.

236 Robert Morley, C.B.E., Actor and Dramatist.

237 Lord Morris of Borth-y-Gest, C.H., C.B.E., M.C., A Lord of Appeal.

238 Sir Brian Morton, F.R.I.C.S., Chairman, Londonderry Development Commission, 1969–73; Chairman, Harland and Wolff, since 1975.

239 Air Vice-Marshal Leslie Moulton, C.B., D.F.C., F.R.S.A., Air Officer Commanding, No. 90 (Signals) Group, Royal Air Force, 1969–71.

240 Richard Murdoch, Stage, Film, Radio and Television Actor.

241 Lieut.-Colonel Sir Edmund Neville, Bt., M.C., Commander, Light Infantry Training Centre, 1941–44.

242 Viscount Newport, Landowner.

243 Lieut.-General Lord Norrie, G.C.M.G., G.C.V.O., C.B., D.S.O., M.C., Governor, South Australia, 1944–51; Governor-General and C.-in-C. New Zealand, 1952–57; Chancellor, Order of St. Michael and St. George, 1960–68.

244 Sir Arthur Norrington, M.A., J.P., Secretary to the Delegates, Oxford University Press, 1948–54; President, Trinity College, Oxford, 1954–70; Vice-Chancellor, Oxford University, 1950–52.

246 Lord O'Neill of the Maine, D.L., Prime Minister of Northern Ireland, 1963–69.

245 Professor C. W. Ottaway, Ph.D., F.R.C.V.S., Emeritus Professor of Veterinary Science, University of Bristol.

247 Sir Duncan Oppenheim, Formerly Chairman, British-American Tobacco Co. Ltd.

249 Sir Anthony Part, G.C.B., M.B.E., Permanent Secretary, Department of Industry, 1974–76.

250 Michael Pattrick, C.B.E., F.R.I.B.A., A.A.Dipl., Principal, Central School of Art and Design, since 1961.

248 Sir Rudolf Peierls, C.B.E., M.A., D.Sc., D.Phil., F.R.S., Wykeham Professor of Physics, University of Oxford, 1963–74.

252 Michael Pertwee, Playwright and Screenwriter.

251 Professor Owen Hood Phillips, D.C.L., M.A., LL.M., Q.C., J.P., Legal Writer; Formerly Dean of the Faculty of Law, University of Birmingham.

253 Wilfred Pickles, O.B.E., Actor and Broadcaster.

254 Sir Hubert Pitman, O.B.E., Sheriff of the City of London, 1959–60.

255 Judge M. George Polson, Q.C., Recorder of Exeter and Chairman of Isle of Wight Quarter Sessions, 1966–71; Member, General Council of the Bar, 1967–70; Circuit Judge and Honorary Recorder of Exeter, since 1972.

256 Surgeon Rear-Admiral Arnold Ashworth Pomfret, C.B., O.B.E., Former Royal Navy Ophthalmic Specialist.

257 Admiral Sir Reginald Portal, K.B.E., D.S.C.

258 Sir Hilton Poynton, G.C.M.G., Permanent Under-Secretary of State, Colonial Office, 1959–66; Director, Overseas Branch, St. John Ambulance, 1968–75.

259 The Rt. Hon. Reg Prentice, J.P., M.P., Minister for Overseas Development, since 1975.

260 J. B. Priestley, M.A., Litt.D., LL.D., D.Litt., Author.

261 Colonel Sir Steuart Pringle, Bt., Colonel, General Staff, Headquarters Commando Forces, Royal Marines, since 1974.

262 Brigadier Sir Otho Prior-Palmer, D.S.O., Member of Parliament for Worthing, 1945–64.

263 The Hon. Terence Prittie, M.B.E., Author and Journalist; Escaped six times when P.O.W. Germany.

264 Harry Rabinowitz, Musical Director, Conductor and Composer.

265 Steve Race, A.R.A.M., Broadcaster and Musician.

266 Sir Alex Randall, K.C.M.G., O.B.E., Diplomat; H.M. Ambassador to Denmark, 1945–52.

268 Ted Ray, Actor and Comedian.

267. Sir Paul Reilly, Director, Design Council, since 1960; Chief Executive, Crafts Advisory Committee, since 1971.

269 Sir Eric Richardson, C.B.E., Ph.D., B.Eng., F.P.S., F.R.S.A., Director, The Polytechnic of Central London, 1969–70.

270 Sir Ralph Richardson, Actor; President of the National Youth Theatre and Greater London Arts Association.

271 Arnold Ridley, Author, Playwright, Actor and Producer.

272 C. H. Rolph, Author and Journalist; Director, New Statesman.

273 Sir Ashton Roskill, Q.C., M.A., Chairman, Monopolies and Mergers Commission, 1965–75.

152

274 Lord Rowallan, K.T., K.B.E., M.C., T.D., D.L., Chief Scout, British Commonwealth and Empire, 1945–59; Governor of Tasmania, 1959–63.

276 Sir Frederick Russell, C.B.E., D.S.C., D.F.C., F.R.S., Marine Biologist, Secretary, Marine Biological Association of the United Kingdom, 1945–65.

275 Sir Harold Sanders, M.A., Ph.D., Chief Scientific Adviser, Ministry of Agriculture, Fisheries and Food, 1955–64.

277 Lord Sandhurst, D.F.C., Wine Shipper.

278 Sir Donald Sargent, K.B.E., C.B., Secretary, National Assistance Board and Supplementary Benefits Commission, 1959–68; Chairman, Civil Service Retirement Fellowship, 1968–74.

279 Vice-Admiral John Scatchard, C.B., D.S.C., Flag Officer, Second-in-Command, Far East Fleet, 1962–64.

280 Lord Simon of Glaisdale, D.L., President, Probate, Divorce and Admiralty Division of the High Court of Justice, 1962–71; a Lord of Appeal, since 1971.

281 General Sir Frank Simpson, G.B.E., K.C.B., D.S.O., Commandant, Imperial Defence College, 1952–54; Chief Royal Engineer, 1961–67.

282 Marshal of the Royal Air Force Sir John Slessor, G.C.B., D.S.O., M.C., Chief of the Air Staff, 1950–52.

285 Barry Granger Smallman, C.V.O., Diplomat; British High Commissioner to Bangladesh, since 1975.

286 Professor Sir David Smithers, M.D., F.R.C.P., F.R.C.S., F.R.C.R., Professor of Radiotherapy in the University of London, 1943–73.

283 Sir Lionel Smith-Gordon, Bt., Writer and Translator.

284 Air Vice-Marshal Frederick B. Sowrey, C.B., C.B.E., A.F.C., Director-General of Royal Air Force Training.

287 Graham Henry Stainforth, Headmaster of Oundle, 1945–56; Master of Wellington College, 1956–66.

288 Air Vice-Marshal William P. Stamm, C.B.E., F.R.C.P., F.R.C.Path., Director, Amoebiasis Diagnostic and Research Unit, St. Giles Hospital, Camberwell, London.

289 Brigadier Sir Alexander Stanier, Bt., D.S.O., M.C., D.L., J.P., Lieutenant-Colonel Commanding Welsh Guards, 1945–48.

290 David Steel, M.P., Leader of the Liberal Party.

291 Sir Peter Studd, G.B.E., Lord Mayor of London, 1970–71.

292 The Right Hon. Jeremy Thorpe, M.P., Leader of the Liberal Party, 1967–76.

293 Sir Herbert Todd, C.I.E., Indian Political Service, 1921–47.

294 Sir George Trevelyan, Bt., Warden, Shropshire Adult College, 1947–71.

295 Air Vice-Marshal Stanley Vincent, C.B., D.F.C., A.F.C., D.L., Air Officer Commanding No. 11 Group, Royal Air Force, 1948–50.

296 Lord Wallace of Campsie, K.St.J., J.P., D.L., Industrialist; Past-President, Glasgow Chamber of Commerce.

297 Judge Martyn Ward, a Circuit Judge, since 1972.

300 Lord Wigg, Chairman, Horserace Betting Levy Board, 1967–72.

298 Lord Williamson, C.B.E., J.P., General Secretary, National Union of General and Municipal Workers, 1946–61.

299 The Rt. Hon. Arthur Woodburn, D.Litt., Politician and Writer; Member of Parliament for Clackmannan, 1939–70.

301 The Rt. Hon. George Woodcock, C.B.E., General Secretary, Trades Union Congress, 1960–69.

302 Air Marshal Sir Peter Wykeham, K.C.B., D.S.O., O.B.E., D.F.C., A.F.C., Deputy Chief of the Air Staff, 1967–69.

303 Lord Wylie, V.R.D., Advocate; Senator of the College of Justice in Scotland, since 1974.

Index

"just in case," 107–108

languages, merits of, 28
lawyers, 10, 95
lion, man-eating, 46
Liquor
  evils of, 116
  intake of, 21, 46, 87, 90, 98, 100, 106, 115, 131
  knowledge of, 46
  longevity and, 90; *see* drinking
little boy, 8, 22, 31, 48, 72, 118
little girl, 72, 91, 129
longevity, 97
lumberjacks, 40–41

marriage, 27
Marx, Groucho, 39
measured collision, 65
Medical
  doctor, 18, 37, 74, 80, 84, 95, 120, 130, 137
  psychiatrist, 7, 61, 116–117
  psychoanalyst, 58–59
Member of Parliament, 15
military, 8, 11, 17, 75, 85–86
Military officer, 8
monastery, 9
money, 10, 20, 28, 51, 52, 83, 89–90, 109, 116, 125
monk, 9
Monteux, Pierre, 37
mouse, 78
music, 7, 92, 93–94
mynah, 30

Navy, British, 7, 67, 68–69, 86, 93
nudity, 16, 105–106; *see also,* sex

old-age wisdom, 34, 37
Old Clergyman, 18
Oxford College, an, 52

parental obedience, 22
parking, 66
parrot, talking, 11–12
parsimony, 16, 19, 61
party, birthday, 60
patriotism, 11
"pays to advertize," 71
Peer, old hereditary, 32
penguin, 31, 66
physicist, 21
physics, laws of, 36–37, 101–103
pigeon, 55
pilot, 10
poetry-reciting mynah bird, 30
policeman, 8
politicians, 15, 34, 37, 47, 56, 76
porridge, 39
prayer, 17
pregnancy, 122
press, the, 59
prisoner, 12
professor, 22, 77
prunes, 22
psychiatrist, *see* Medical
psychoanalyst, *see* Medical

rabbit, 25